SEVENTY WEEKS
THE HISTORICAL ALTERNATIVE

SEVENTY WEEKS
THE HISTORICAL ALTERNATIVE

ROBERT CARINGOLA

FOREWORD BY
CHARLES A. JENNINGS

TRUTH IN HISTORY

P.O. BOX 808

OWASSO, OK 74055-0808

WWW.TRUTHINHISTORY.ORG

Dedication

This book, *Seventy Weeks: The Historical Alternative*, is dedicated to the memory of the late Rev. David Campbell, minister of Life Tabernacle Pentecostal Church, Farringdon, Sunderland, England. In 1981, this pillar in Christ's glorious Kingdom forever changed my life and my prophetic understanding. I have known no other minister who could walk in his shoes.

70 Weeks
Robert Caringola
Kingdom Treasure Ministries, Inc.

ISBN-13 978-1-56043-445-0

Contents

ECCLESIASTES 12:10

The preacher sought to find out acceptable words: and that which was written was upright, even words of truth.

REV. DAVID CAMPBELL

We get two feet to follow others with. We get a brain to think for ourselves. And I can follow them better with my two feet if my brain is satisfied. And when my brain is satisfied, then my heart is satisfied.

Foreword

Courage was a sterling quality within the character of many Biblical personalities of both the Old and New Testaments. It took courage for the Prophet Daniel to resist the edicts of a wicked king, or Jeremiah when denouncing the sins of the Judah nation and prophesied of national judgment when all the other 'prophets' of his day were crying peace and safety.

In his book, "Seventy Weeks", Robert Caringola displays that same quality of courage as he deals with an extremely important theological topic which is generally misunderstood and even abused by most theologians today. The Seventy Weeks of Daniel has been so abused and misused by Futurist prophecy "experts" that in many cases it has constituted the raping of sacred Scripture. In their ignorance, but most often, their deliberate blindness, the modern prophecy "experts" continue to espouse the lifeless theories of the Jesuits and their evangelical converts.

In his plain and straightforward approach, the author clearly explains the truth of Scripture that was once known and believed by the saints of long-ago and the stalwarts of the Protestant Reformation. His sincere attempt is to clarify to each reader the truth of the greatest and most significant Messianic prophecy found within the pages of the Canon of divinely inspired Scripture. It took Godly courage for Robert to follow the plain teaching of Scriptural prophecy and then to print it within the pages of this book as a modern day witness to the historic belief of the Christian Church. In this modern religious environment when cowardice has invaded the pulpit, the Historicist approach to the study of eschatology is a bold return to the faith of the ancient Hebrew Prophets, the first-century Apostles and the fathers of the Protestant Reformation.

Traditionally, the battle for divine truth has sometimes been fought in bloody trenches with sword and spear and within the wall of seminaries with both tongue and pen. Regardless of the physical venue of the battle, the real war rages within the minds and hearts of men as they search for divine nuggets hidden within the pages of Holy Scripture. Every sincere and humble servant of Jesus, the Master Teacher, is willing for their doctrinal and prophetic perspectives to be brought in line with Divine Revelation when exposed under the spotlight of truth. Man-made religious traditions and beliefs must submit to the infallible words of God's Apostles and Prophets as they were moved by the Holy Ghost.

The battle for truth today is not fought on a bloody field nor confined within the walls of academia, but the battle now rages throughout our religious and social culture of Western Civilization. Unfortunately, the words of Aeschylus, the Greek dramatist, are ever so true when he wrote; "In war, truth is the first casualty." Far too long the true understanding of the greatest Messianic prophecy ever proclaimed by God's anointed prophets has been the casualty in the theological and cultural war for truth. The prophetic insight given to the Prophet Daniel near the end of the seventy years of exile in Babylon was the most profound witness to the Judah nation proving that Jesus Christ was the promised Messiah of Israel. The religious blindness of the Jewish leaders of that day prevented their understanding of God's greatest Messianic timeline, yet that same blindness has also prevailed among teachers of prophetic futurism today.

Sad to say, the prophecy which speaks of the grandeur and beauty of the Messiah's first coming has been attributed to some make-believe 'antichrist' of the future. The prophecy which clearly proclaims Christ in all His ineffable accomplishments at Calvary, are attributed by the Futurist prophecy gurus as pertaining to some evil 'boogeyman' now lurking in the dark shadows of an unseen evil empire, ready to be revealed after the so-called rapture of the Church.

At the age of thirty at His water baptism, our Lord knew that the Seventieth Week of Daniel was at its commencement when He told His followers; ***"The time is fulfilled, and the Kingdom of God is at hand:"*** (Mark 1:15). At this point it was time for His public ministry to begin just as the Prophet Daniel declared. The timing of the fulfillment of this prophecy alone was enough to prove to that unbelieving generation that Jesus was the promised Messiah. That is how important the Seventy Week prophecy was to that age and still stands as a monument to the authenticity of Divine Revelation as recorded in our Bible.

In this book, Robert sets forth the clear and irrefutable facts of correct prophetic interpretation that are available to every student seeking Biblical truth who is willing to lay aside thumb-worn religious creeds for the fresh and living bread of Divine insight. Within these pages you will be challenged to take an honest look once again at the Prophet Daniel's most important vision of Messianic significance.

It is past time in this battle for eschatological understanding that ministers and laymen alike return to the inspired utterance of the Apostles and Prophets. It is also time to discard the various empty speculations of men who are constantly on the prowl in their search for an 'antichrist' that would be a suitable candidate to fulfill their latest prognostication.

In exposing the falsehood of dispensational futurism, the author of this book has done a great service to all Christendom by bringing to the light of day the Historicist viewpoint which has been pushed out of reach of most Christians by misguided 'men of the cloth.' The erudite Presbyterian pastor and Bible expositor, Matthew Henry once said, "Truth seeks no corners, however it may sometime be forced into them."

God's truth is seemingly always on trial in the court of man's theological jurisdiction, but "Truth seeks neither place nor applause, bows to no human shrine, possesses neither fear nor favor, all she asks, is a hearing."

It is my honor to have a part in making this edition of "Seventy Weeks" available to this end-time generation as a bright light shining forth in a dark world of "futuristic" prophetic fiction. My prayer is that students of the prophetic Scriptures will once again understand the greatest Messianic prophecy which so clearly portrays the glory and splendor of our beloved Savior.

Charles A. Jennings

Truth in History

Preface

H. Grattan Guinness, England's great teacher of Bible prophecy, wrote these words of rebuke to those who dare to teach what they know not:

> *A wide distinction exists and should be recognized between* ***students and expositors of the Word and Works of God*** *who humbly, soberly and reverently search into the facts of Nature and Scripture, of providence and prophecy, reach conclusions which sanctified common sense can approve, and* ***speculators****, who, running away with isolated and mysterious expressions, indulge in imaginations of their own and become prophets, instead of students of Divine prophecy.*

In 1981, I was shocked into the realization that I was nothing more than a "speculator" when it came to teaching Bible prophecy. This revelation occurred while I was providentially sitting under the prophetic presentation ministry of English minister David Campbell. He taught for three hours on Bible prophecy, specifically, the seventy weeks of Daniel chapter nine, in which he presented the history and origin of the various interpretations of prophecy. Every minister present at this seminar was overwhelmed at this teacher's anointing and knowledge of the Scriptures. David clearly presented the Protestant historical alternative to the present preeminent school of eschatology known as "dispensationalism." In that stunning three-hour seminar, all of our Clarence Larkin and Hal Lindsey theories were put to the test and burned up before our eyes. All of our sensational prophetic expressions crumbled before clear biblical truth. David presented the works of some of the greatest teachers who have ever written on Bible prophecy, such as the Rev. E.B. Elliott, author of the epic ***Horae Apocalypticae;*** H. Grattan Guinness, author of ***The Approaching End of the Age,*** and Bishop Thomas Newton's ***Dissertations on the Prophecies.*** I had never seen these men's historical perspectives mentioned in any of the eschatological books I had ever studied. Now I understand why. I left that seminar with the burning witness of the Holy Ghost deep within the eyes of my understanding, crying out, "What meaneth this?"

At the seminar, many of the historically consistent keys of knowledge pertaining to the study of the written prophets were imparted. Afterward, I felt I had no alternative but to intensely study the great Protestant historical interpretation of Bible prophecy. This wasn't easy, since so many of the great writings were not readily accessible. Nevertheless, God provided, and I began a journey to prove the things which had been taught that spectacular summer day. After a decade of study, I am convinced that truth will again triumph in the volatile arena of eschatology, and shortly we will return to prophetic teachings that reveal the progressive nature of the Kingdom of God as it grows from a stone to a mountain and fills the whole earth![1] The more I studied the Protestant historical interpretation (historicism), the more I became convinced of its consistent truth and its ability to once again assert the credibility of God's Word upon His written prophets. As the story began to unfold and the interpretation became sure, I purposed in my heart to cry out as Luther did when he made his great, providential stand for truth in 1521 before the Holy Roman Emperor Charles V at the Diet of Worms, Germany. (Hei shehe ich. Ich kan nicht anders. Got helffe mir. Amen) "Here I stand. I cannot do otherwise. God help me."[2] I was becoming increasingly aware of the dangers of the dispensationalist teachings in eschatology (also known as ***futurism***), and of how these teachings were perverting our Lord's revelation of Himself.

But now I rejoice because the folly of dispensationalism, its erroneous predictions, themes and calculated dates, is beginning to pass on the wind of summer's threshing floor. However, I am not naive enough to think that it will fall without a fight; therefore, a sharp offensive sword must be unsheathed throughout this book. I cannot rejoice in the multitude of saints who are, and will be, left in the scorching heat of confusion. It is for these that I risk writing this controversial book. Christ is opening a great door for truth, and be assured truth will triumph. I hope to repair this terrible breach in the study of the written prophets, along with other men of knowledge and courage.

It will become quite clear that there is no neutrality on my part as I work through this brief historical chronology and exegesis on the great prophecy of Daniel chapter nine. The idea of neutrality does not stand before firm Berean scrutiny. We all must speak from a given perspective. I will write from a perspective that has survived both the fiery hell of opposition and the bloodletting attacks of the diabolically deceived. Someone has said, "When truth is established, objections are nothing; for one is founded on knowledge, and the other on ignorance." This work is birthed with the intent of establishing truth and subsequently freeing men's minds from the "terrible curse of uncertainty," to quote Martin Luther.

---

1 Daniel 2:35

2 Roland H. Bainton, *Here I Stand: A Life of Martin Luther*, p. 145.

"I have sworn upon the altar of God eternal hostility against every form of tyranny over the mind of men," wrote Thomas Jefferson in a letter to his friend Benjamin Rush. Any form of false biblical teaching is a form of vicious tyranny over the minds of God's flock. The little-known tyranny involved in destroying the historical coherency of Daniel's epochal time measure, recorded in chapter nine of his prophecy, will be revealed in this book. I pray that the reader patiently follow the story as it unfolds. If this book can prove that the Divine time measure of the seventy weeks is already totally fulfilled in history, then everything must change in our understanding of eschatology. The ***parenthesis theory*** of the seventy weeks is the pillar of futurism. I intend to expose this erroneous assumption using clear biblical and historical truth. God help me!

Rousas John Rushdoony shared in his book, ***God's Plan for Victory***, a very sobering thought concerning differing doctrines of eschatology:

> *Once we adopt a position, it has certain logical consequences and also very practical implications for our lives. If I believe that Christ will soon rapture me from this evil world, this will have a practical effect on my life very different from a belief that I shall see the world get worse and worse, and live through a fearful tribulation. Again, if I believe that the world will see the progressive triumph of Christ's people until the whole world is Christian and a glorious material and spiritual era unfolds, I shall be motivated very much differently. Thus we cannot hold that these differing doctrines of eschatology [the study of last things] are a matter of indifference. They make a very great difference in how we view the world and our work and future in it...our view of the end, of eschatology, depends to a large measure on our view of the beginning, and of all history, and our doctrine of God and salvation.*

Could this man's observations be correct? Do eschatological interpretations make a difference, or does anything go in this arena? I assure you that his perspective is correct (although his prophetic theology may not be). In this systematic teaching, I intend to take this premise much further. I will endeavor to answer these fundamental questions: How did the chaos in eschatology begin? What is the history behind what we've been taught, and can anyone coherently bring this message into an even place? Must we be doomed to be like Pilate, forever beseeching, "What is truth?" As you read this book, these questions will be addressed and they will be answered. It's not as difficult as you may think.

Acts 3:20-21 states:

And he shall send Jesus Christ, which before was preached unto

you: Whom the heaven must receive until the times of restitution* [restoration] *of all things, which God hath spoken by the mouth of all his holy prophets since the world began.

I have no doubt that we are living in a very special time. It is evident that we were born for such an hour as this. Much truth is being restored to the body of Christ. I believe that this foretold restoration is manifesting itself in a multitude of witnesses. For example, God is restoring truth about the five-fold ministry in His Kingdom. Likewise, the truth of this ***present*** Kingdom is being revealed throughout the body of Christ. Jesus told the Jews, ***"Therefore say I unto you, The kingdom of God shall be taken from you, and given to a nation bringing forth the fruits thereof."***[3] Christ was not talking about some phenomenon restricted to a great millennium yet to come. This Kingdom was present and, according to Daniel, it will grow and fill the earth! It is not going down in defeat to some antichrist! Also, God will restore the truth of the Protestant interpretation of Bible prophecy (historicism). This proven, yet forgotten, systematic interpretation will reinstate our linear historical perspective. We, like great men in the past, will again be able to look into the Book of Revelation and define our place in its grand panoramic prophecy, thus putting our feet on a solid rock of interpretation.

Finally, I run a great risk by exposing, and attacking when necessary, doctrinal teachers from ***historic*** Roman Catholicism. I have no option but to assume this risk, and let it possibly bring forth its fruit. God will be my Refuge and my Strength; in Him will I trust. Why is this necessary? You will be shocked to discover that Rome's Jesuits are responsible for birthing both of the most commonly held eschatological positions taught today. Why did they produce these theologies? If you read this book you will surely be enlightened. Be Berean when you study! I'll never forget reading the following statement, relevant to attitudes one must avoid if he wants to increase in the knowledge and understanding of the Scriptures:

There is a principle which is a bar against all information, which is proof against all argument, and which cannot fail to keep a man or woman in everlasting ignorance. This principle is contempt prior to investigation.

The Scriptures state:

He who answereth a matter before he heareth it, it is folly and shame unto him.[3]

---

3 Proverbs 18:13

And, my friend, take comfort in the fact that...

We have also a more sure word of prophecy; whereunto ye do well that ye take heed...knowing this first, that no prophecy of the scripture is of any private interpretation.[4]

Having said all this, I do, as the author, take total responsibility for the shortcomings of this book. There is, of necessity, periodically incomplete exegesis in order to clarify the book's main theme. I have attempted to be as wise and scholastic as possible when doing so. I pray that the reader will understand.

4 II Peter 1:19-20

Part One
Setting the Stage

Seventy Weeks: The Vision

The prophecy of the seventy weeks is one of the most spectacular Divine time measures in Holy Writ. Prophecy consists of God showing us history (His story) in advance, and a Divine time measure is a prophecy which is confined to a specific amount of time in which the events prophesied must come to pass without error. God has often used this tool in His Word to assert the credibility of the written prophetic. Only the God of the Bible has been able to encapsulate history within the confines of His foretold will. Thus He establishes His power and authority over all. Remember, God views the complexity of nations as just a ***"drop of a bucket"*** (Isa. 40:15). The seventy weeks reveal to mankind the exact year that ***Messiah the Prince***[5] came, appearing on the earth in His public ministry. This is truly amazing. Let's define the scenario around the impartation of this prophecy concerning the Jews to Daniel, the Babylonian captive.

In the year 538 B.C. the prophet and interpreter of dreams Daniel, received from the angel Gabriel the vision of the seventy weeks. As previously stated, this word is one of the greatest Messianic prophecies in the Scriptures. It perfectly identified the year (27 A.D.) in which Messiah the Prince would appear and begin His earthly ministry, confirming the New Covenant with Daniel's people (the Jews) for one week (i.e., seven years). Also, this same year (538 B.C.) marked the beginning of the Jews' restoration and deliverance from exile by the decree of the victorious Cyrus, king of the new Medo-Persian empire and conqueror of Babylon.[6] The vision of the seventy weeks is recorded as follows:

DANIEL 9:24-27

v.24 Seventy weeks are determined [or served off, R.V.] upon thy holy city [Jerusalem].

1. *To finish the transgression;*
2. *To make an end of sins;*
3. *To make reconciliation for iniquity;*
4. *To bring in everlasting righteousness;*
5. *To seal up the vision and prophecy;*

---

5 Daniel 9:25

6 Ezra 1:1-4

6. *To anoint the most Holy.*

*v.25 Know therefore and understand, that from the going forth of the commandment to restore and to build Jerusalem unto Messiah the Prince [**Son of God**] shall be seven weeks, and threescore and two weeks: the street shall be built again, and the wall, even in troublous times.*

*v.26 And after threescore and two weeks shall Messiah [**Jesus**] be cut off, but not for himself: and the people of the prince that shall come shall destroy the city and the sanctuary; and the end thereof shall be with a flood, and unto the end of the war desolations are determined.*

v.27 And he shall confirm the covenant with many for one week: and in the midst of the week he shall cause the sacrifice and the oblation to cease, and for the overspreading of abominations he shall make it desolate, even unto the consummation, and that determined shall be poured upon the desolate.

So while Daniel was speaking, praying and confessing both his sin and that of his captive people Israel, Gabriel came before him and presented what centuries later will be known as indisputable proof that Jesus Christ was this foretold Messiah the Prince. Only Jesus precisely fulfilled this prophecy.

In order to further enhance our historical perspective, let's briefly outline the sequence of Gentile empires as listed in Daniel chapter two. This was Nebuchadnezzar's vision of the golden image, properly interpreted as five kingdoms which would rule consecutively in the prophetic earth.

Nebuchadnezzar, king of Babylon, had an extremely important dream. He refused to inform his "wise men" of its contents, yet he put the burden of interpretation on them! He demanded the exact revelation and interpretation. They responded, ***"It is a rare thing that the king requireth, and there is none other that can shew it before the king, except the gods, whose dwelling is not with flesh."***[7] Wrong, false prophets, the God of Heaven does dwell with men! As we know, Daniel was able to reveal the content of the dream and give its interpretation. Following is an outline of Nebuchadnezzar's dream.

---

7 Daniel 2:11

NEBUCHADNEZZAR'S GREAT IMAGE

HEAD OF GOLD (Babylon 741-538 B.C.)

BREAST AND ARMS OF SILVER (Medo-Persia 538-336 B.C.)

BELLY AND THIGHS OF BRASS (Greece 336-62 B.C.)

LEGS OF IRON (Rome [pagan] 62 B.C.-313 A.D.)

FEET & TOES OF IRON AND CLAY (Rome sub-divided 476 A.D.)

By looking at the historical chronology of the vision, we can identify the empire, in relation to the others, in which the Divine time measure of the seventy weeks commenced. Daniel's seventy weeks began in the days of the Medo-Persian empire, under the reign of King Artaxerxes I. The time measure began in the year 457 B.C.

Many try to begin the time measure with the decree of Cyrus in 538 B.C. This will be addressed in detail. This is an indiscretion that many well-intentioned students of Bible prophecy have made. We are going to be examining a Divine time measure that identifies the exact year Messiah the Prince (Jesus Christ) began His earthly ministry. We cannot have an 81-year mistake in our calculations!

The confusion in determining which decree, Cyrus' or Artaxerxes', marked the starting point for the seventy weeks is only one of the major problems we face. The other is the exact ending of the prophecy (its fulfillment). I am asserting that this great prophetic continuum of the Bible has run its course completely. I will reveal the event that ended its exclusive application to Daniel's people (the Jews), and establish, with the force of Scripture, that Christ has fulfilled all six Messianic prophecies contained therein.

The other problem on the stage of history is the genesis of the interpretation most widely held today. Where did it come from? Why was it written? And how was it treated by great men of God for centuries? The proper eschatological term for the view most taught today is ***Futurism.***[8] It is futuristic eschatology which fuels the confusion of ***Dispensationalism.***[9] The futuristic school of Bible prophecy came

---

8 "Futurists...would relate the predictions of John's volume [and Daniel's last week, i.e. seven years] to events which have not yet occurred. When consistently applied, futurism treats even the details that are suggested about the seven churches of Asia as unfulfilled prophecy." J. Barton Payne, *Encyclopedia of Biblical Prophecy*, p. 593.

9 "With the rise of the Plymouth Brethren movement under J.N. Darby in the 1820's, dispensational premillennialism has attained a wide following among modern evangelicals. It is distinguished by its insistence that the O.T. prophecies are to receive their literal fulfillment in the restored polity of Israel after the flesh, rather than in the Church [this teaching is enhanced by the so-called seven year tribulation period, which comes from the futurists breaking Daniel's Divine time measure]." Ibid, p. 59.

from the Roman Catholic church, specifically her Jesuit theologians. This actuality has been a known and documented truth in the Protestant church for centuries, and it is the interpretation held by the vast majority of Christians today. However, the alternative has been believed for centuries. It is known as ***Historicism.***[10]

10 "Historicalists, including the majority of Protestant interpreters up to the 19th century, discovered within the Revelation a full sweep of Church history, often with amazing details on Mohammed, the papacy, Napoleon, etc." Ibid, p. 593.

Different Interpretations?

I once talked with a young man about the great Protestant Reformation of the 16th century. Although he had been part of the Christian community for about twenty years, a few minutes into the conversation, I realized that he was not comprehending what I was telling him. I asked, "Do you know what I'm talking about when I speak of the Reformation?" His answer was a pathetically sincere "No." I was shocked; probably more disgusted. How could this brother have no fundamental grasp of history? Was he responsible for this dangerous ignorance, or were the teachers who instructed him the guilty party? In his case I didn't know.

Christianity is essentially a historical religion. Our Bible is full of history. Most parts of the Scriptures cannot be understood without a foundational knowledge and grasp of historical events and themes. Without this weapon of understanding we sit in a very vulnerable position. The prophet Hosea clearly warned us of this danger:

> *My people are destroyed for lack of knowledge: because thou hast rejected knowledge, I will also reject thee, that thou shalt be no priest to me: seeing thou hast forgotten the law of thy God, I will also forget thy children.*[11]

It seems as though every time history tries to repeat itself, and we are void of the knowledge necessary to interpret it, the price doubles. In the study of eschatology, are we historically armed? Do we really know where all the various interpretations came from? Were these honest men trying their best to understand difficult passages of Scripture, or are we dealing with something much more sinister? As we look at some amazing beliefs in the Church, some older than a millennium, ask yourself, "Why haven't I been told this?" "Why haven't I been given a chance to study the alternative for myself?" "What is going on here?" Let's start our brief investigation in the second century with Irenaeus, the grand pupil of the Apostle John.

Irenaeus believed that the antichrist would arise in the Church and be identified as a religious apostate. What caused him to believe this? The answer is found in First John 2:18-19, which states:

> *Little children, it is the last time: and as ye have heard that antichrist shall come, even now are there many antichrists; whereby we know*

11 Hosea 4:6

that it is the last time. ***They went out from us****, but they were not of us for if they had been of us; they would no doubt have continued with us: but they went out, that they might be made manifest that they were not all of us.*

Do you understand what is said here? The Antichrist must be a religious apostate! He will not be some secular political figure. It could not be simpler. Antichrist must come out from true Christianity and manifest himself as an apostate. Also, Irenaeus taught that the great subject of the apocalyptic Beast, Antichrist, would arise after the division of the pagan Roman empire into ten kingdoms, as that which would immediately precede, and then be followed by, Antichrist's manifestation.[12] And finally, he knew that this man would manifest himself out of the Latin Kingdom. The understanding was that the Antichrist, Man of Sin, the Wicked One, or the Little Horn of Daniel chapter seven (all the same apostasy) would rise out of the Latin culture. Irenaeus thought that Antichrist would be a Latin man, with the Latin language, from the Latin Kingdom.[13]

Next we turn to Tertullian. On the subject of Antichrist,[14] he agreed with Irenaeus in expecting events to develop chronologically after the breaking up of the Roman Empire into ten kings, or kingdoms.[15]

Thirdly, coming into brief mention is Hippolytus, Bishop of Porto. He was an immediate successor of Irenaeus and Tertullian. It is understood that he was Irenaeus' disciple. Elliott states that Hippolytus' Treatise on Antichrist had "every mark of genuineness." He, like his two apostolic fathers, believed that the designative title "Antichrist" would apply to the Latin Man.[16]

So we have seen three Pre-Nicean fathers who all agreed that the coming apostasy would arise from Rome. Later we will examine the great prophetic riddle of Revelation 17:9-12 (the Seven Kings), to further see how these men could have such amazingly accurate prophetic insight.

Furthermore, their interpretation of Paul's writing to the church of Thessalonica concerning what would hinder the rise of the great apostasy was quite different than what is being taught today. The Scripture states,

---

12 Rev. E.B. Elliott, A.M., Horae Apocalypticae, "History of Apocalyptic Interpretation," vol. 4, p. 278.

13 Cathcart' The Papal System, p. 389-391.

14 Horae Apocalypticae, p. 279.

15 Daniel 7:7

16 Horae Apocalypticae, vol. 4, p. 282-285.

"He who now letteth [being interpreted 'hinder' (old Anglo-Saxon word meaning 'not to allow')] will let, until he be taken out of the way."[17] This was understood to mean the Roman Emperors and their empire. Again, this knowledge came partly from Revelation 17:9-12. Elliott writes:

> *We have the consenting testimony of the early Fathers, from Irenaeus, the disciple of John, to the effect that it (hindrance) was understood to be the Imperial power ruling and residing in Rome.*[18]

So, we ask ourselves, are these different interpretations, or are they a consistent school of thought that reigned sovereign in the minds of God's servants until the latter part of the 19th century?

It is not so well known that all the reformers believed these basic points and attached the title "antichrist" to the papacy. Thirteen centuries after Irenaeus, Christians still looked at Rome through the refining fire of the Word of God, and they exposed her! This teaching was a pillar of truth in the Reformation. As a matter of fact, it was the only doctrine so self-evident that all the reformers could accept the interpretation! Luther and Calvin were not restrained when it came to exposing the leader of the great apostasy. Luther wrote:

> *We are of the conviction that the papacy is the seat of the true and real Antichrist...personally I declare that I owe the Pope no other obedience than that to Antichrist.*[19]

Martin Luther wrote this in 1520, and it is understood that he was speaking of a system, not just Pope Leo X. He did not hastily come to this conclusion, but his conscience bore intense witness to the truths he was uncovering. The great French Reformer, John Calvin, was not timid when it came to this subject either. His position is defined in his classic Institutes, in which he states:

> *Some persons think us too severe and censorious when we call the Roman Pontiff Antichrist. But those who are of this opinion do not consider that they bring the same charge of presumption against Paul himself after whom we speak and whose language we adopt...*[20]

Calvin, like Luther, had no problem with consistently interpreting Daniel's, Paul's and John's teachings on antichrist. The contemporary historian and reconstructionist, Dr. Gary North, likewise recognizes

---

17 II Thessalonians 2:7

18 Horae, Apocalypticae, vol. 3, p. 92.

19 Froom, The Prophetic Faith of Our Fathers, vol. 2, p. 121.

20 Ralph Woodrow, Great Prophecies of the Bible, p. 186.

their oneness of thought. He writes:

> *Church historicism teaches that the Book of Revelation describes the course of history. This was the common view of the Reformation, in which all Protestant groups identified the Papacy as the antichrist.* ***(This was the only universally agreed-upon specifically Protestant doctrine that united all Protestant groups. [emphasis mine])***[21]

What does all this have to do with the seventy weeks? My friend, it has everything to do with it. It was because of the Reformation that Rome went to Daniel chapter nine in an attempt to try to protect the papacy from the piercing accusations of the Protestants. As we further examine a few more "different interpretations," we will begin to discern the difference between our present day teachings and the teachings which were strength and wisdom to the Church for centuries.

Since we are examining the theme of antichrist, let us see why these men viewed this apostasy as a dynasty, not just a single individual who would reign at the end of time (we'll later discover who first taught this view).

King Nebuchadnezzar inquired of Daniel concerning his dream (Daniel 2). He said, "Art thou able to make known unto me the dream which I have seen, and the interpretation thereof?" Daniel answered, "There is a God in heaven that revealeth secrets, and maketh known to the king Nebuchadnezzar what shall be in the latter days." The dream described a great image with a head of gold. Daniel looked firmly at Nebuchadnezzar and said, "Thou art this head of gold." Thus, Nebuchadnezzar symbolized the great empire of Babylon. However, he was not its only king. He represented a dynasty of kings. Likewise, antichrist was understood to be a dynasty of men who would fulfill the role of the "little horn" in Daniel chapter seven, and "persecute the saints of the most high…until a time, and times, and the dividing of time." This is calculated to be 1,260 days. But, as we will discover on our journey for prophetic truth, in prophecies other than the seventy weeks, days can and do stand for years! The "day-for-a-year" truth when interpreting Divine time measures has undergone a literal genocide in prophetic theology. Who first declared war on it? We'll find out later. By then you'll be fairly concerned.

Finally, let's examine one more point that has been interpreted historically much differently than today's prophetic teachers interpret it—the Temple. The teaching of a literal rebuilt Temple in Jerusalem is a bulwark of futuristic eschatology. I believe Hal Lindsey qualifies as the

21 Dr. Kenneth Gentry, The Beast of Revelation 666, p. xii, footnote 5.

preeminent futurist of our time. I can make this statement because we know that he is the most widely read author on this subject. His book, *The Late Great Planet Earth*, was the #1 best seller of the 1980's. He has undoubtedly put himself in the forefront, so let's reference him for a glimpse of futuristic Temple teaching:

> *The Antichrist will deify himself—just like the Caesars did. He will proclaim himself to be God. He will demand that he be worshiped and will establish himself in the Temple of God (II Thess. 2:4).*
>
> *There is only one place where this temple of God can be and that is on Mount Moriah in Jerusalem, on the site where the Dome of the Rock and other Moslem shrines now stand. There are many places in the Bible that pinpoint this location as the one where the Jews will rebuild their Temple.*[22]

Do you understand the message? He wants us to believe that this is a literal Temple. Isn't that strange? It's not only strange, but it's foreign to consistent historical interpretation. The Reformation fathers would gaze upon us with intense bewilderment should we openly espouse this interpretation. They understood only one Temple relevant to the Christian era. We will prove what this Temple is with a simple word study later.

This "stage setting" should have shown that some very fundamental issues in eschatology are at peril. And they need to be. We are on a serious inquiry for truth. Nothing which is not of Christ is sacred. If the test of fire burns it, then Amen.

The next phase of the journey will take us to the Reformation. The real story in eschatology and its various interpretations must originate there. It is in this season of history that the futurist interpretation is birthed from the Roman Catholic Counter-Reformation and her Jesuit theologians. This history must be looked at, and the accusations of the reformers further studied, before we interpret the seventy weeks. We must remember one thing: the doctrine of the Papal Antichrist was a major offensive weapon for the reformers. Multitudes paid a ferocious price for teaching these revolutionary truths. Be assured, God has not forgotten, even though most of His ministers have! [23]

---

22 Hal Lindsey, The Late Great Planet Earth, pp. 109-110.

23 In the APPENDIX, I have recorded the testimony of 16 witnesses to the fact that the Roman Pope is the predicted Man of Sin, the Antichrist. Their testimonies cost several of them their lives. To these men, proclamation of this truth was both necessary and worth their lives—and deaths.

The Reformation

At the opening of the sixteenth century, the Roman Catholic institution was in great peril. She was in her greatest danger since the great schism which occurred between 1378 and 1417. This was a split in the Roman church that occurred immediately after ending the "Babylonian captivity" of the papacy. Two papal lines of authority were completely divided, which resulted in a third contention for power emerging. Also, the theory of the superiority of councils to the pope represented a great danger which challenged the stability of the institution. The secular rulers were suspicious of church policy, and they had great contempt for her leadership. The peasants were infuriated with the excessive financial demands of an immoral clergy. The power of the papacy was being attacked on all sides, and the popes had no military power readily at their command. Moreover, massive debt was taking its toll. And a vast history of persecuting God's saints was catching up with the Catholic church.

The need for reform in the western church was self evident. The corruption and immorality of the vicars of Christ was reaching new heights. Their interest in the secular far outweighed their concerns about the Kingdom of God. A good example is Alexander VI, who used the tithes and offerings of the flock to purchase kingdoms for illegitimate sons. Libraries are full of this remarkable history.

The most frequently voiced complaints were caused by practices that involved the selling of spiritual benefits. Every diabolical form of fund raising was instituted. But the triggering mechanism for reform came in the selling of indulgences.

The Reformation had its beginning when Martin Luther, an Augustinian friar serving as professor of Bible at the University of Wittenberg, wrote ninety-five theses, propositions for academic debate, on the subject of indulgences. An indulgence was a remission of the temporal penalty for sin imposed by a priest in the Roman sacrament of penance. Luther nailed his theses on a church door in Wittenberg on October 31, 1517. He was subsequently excommunicated from the church of Rome, and he left it in 1521.

John Tetzel was the central focus of the indulgence controversy. He was a Dominican monk from Leipzig, who was commissioned by the pope to collect indulgences. Tetzel declared:

Indulgences are the most precious and most noble of God's gifts...1 have saved more souls by my indulgences than the apostle Paul did with his sermons...Indulgences avail not only for the living but for the dead...the moment money clicks at the bottom of the chest the soul departs from purgatory, and flies to heaven. With ten groshen you can deliver your father from purgatory.[24]

"As soon as the coin in the coffer rings the soul from purgatory springs."

Tetzel, Albert of Brandenburg and Pope Leo X were extorting the German population so that St. Peter's Cathedral could be built in Rome.

News of Luther's ninety-five theses exploded throughout Germany. In a very short period of time Rome was forced to respond, and the struggle for truth erupted in Western Christendom. She had underestimated the German professor. It would not be long and much blood would be shed. The Peasant War began in 1525.

Luther started producing tracts and books. As he matured in his understanding, his accusations, accompanied by proof texts, accelerated. His defiance strengthened other men. The course of Western Civilization was being adjusted. In his books, Luther called Rome "Babylon" and the pope, "Antichrist." He and many others were proving this from the Scriptures and history. The fruit on the tree was easy to judge. What is amazing is the multitude of witnesses who have agreed with Luther's prophetic conclusions. We have been taught many of the things these subsequent witnesses believed, but when it comes to Rome, the texts are deleted from contemporary books and likewise, the voice is silent over the pulpit. Here is a brief sampling of other great men of God who believed and expounded these truths:

John Wycliffe
John Knox
William Tyndale
John Calvin
Ulrich Zwingli
Philip Melanchthon
Sir Issac Newton
John Huss
John Foxe
Hugh Latimer
Nicholas Ridley
Thomas Cranmer
John Wesley
Charles Wesley
Jonathan Edwards
George Whitefield
Charles Finney
Charles H. Spurgeon

I could name countless others who refused to be silent when it came

24 J. A. Wylie, History of the Reformation, vol. 1, p. 257.

to the abuses of "Mystery, Babylon the Great."[25] Lengthy quotes and teachings could be produced from all these scholars, both some of the greatest Reformation writers, and others, more recent, men of God.

Luther is considered one of the greatest Protestant scholars who ever lived. He wrote more than any other reformer (this is not well known). He would not whitewash the papacy. He understood the magnitude of deception which had been propagated by the popes and their councils throughout the centuries. We must understand it, as well. If we follow Christ as the Scriptures teach, then this Latin man is not our father! We have no alternative but to warn those who will hear and encourage them to flee from the midst of Babylon! ***"Come out of her, my people, that ye be not partakers of her sins, and that ye receive not of her plagues."***[26]

Luther went further and called the pope the "Son of Perdition." This is an astounding accusation. The word "perdition" is used twice in the New Testament to identify a false apostle. Once it was applied to Judas in John 17:12, where we read, "While I was with them in the world I kept them in thy name: those that thou gavest me I have kept, and none of them is lost, but the son of perdition; that the scripture might be fulfilled." Again, we see the word in Revelation 17:11, which entitled the eighth form of government to arise out of the seven hilled city. "And the beast that was, and is not even he is the eighth, and is of the seven, and goeth into perdition." The application of the term "son of perdition" to the apostolic is an incredible prophecy. As we have seen, Judas received the title; however, it is important to note that even to this day the Roman Catholic church states emphatically that the pope is the only living apostle on earth. This is contained in their doctrine of "apostolic succession." Read the words of the Vatican Council of 1870, which were written under the title, First Dogmatic Constitution on the Church of Christ. Published in the Fourth Session of the Holy Ecumenical Council of the Vatican.

ON THE POWER AND NATURE OF THE PRIMACY OF THE ROMAN PONTIFF

We renew the definition of the Ecumenical Council of Florence, in virtue of which all the faithful of Christ must believe that the Holy Apostolic See and the Roman Pontiff possesses the primacy over the

25 Revelation 17:5

26 Ibid, 18:4

whole world, and that the Roman Pontiff is the successor of Blessed Peter, Prince of the apostles, and is the true Vicar of Christ, and Head of the whole Church, and Father and Teacher of all Christians…[27]

Well, there we have it. An institution that substitutes popes, cardinals, bishops and archbishops, monseigneurs [French, "My Lord"], monks and nuns for the biblical five-fold ministry[28]— apostles, prophets, evangelists, pastors and teachers—trying to assert itself over the teachings of Scripture, cannot be the true Church, Christ's bride. Can you begin to understand the centuries of rage that has been espoused by anointed Protestants? Thank God Luther sowed such good seed.

In 1521, this courageous reformer was brought before the Diet at Worms, Germany. This was the parliament of Charles V, Emperor of the Holy Roman Empire. Luther's books were thrown before him. He asked for twenty-four hours before replying to their charges. His final reply was brief and bold:

> *Since, then, your Serene Majesty and your Lordships ask for a simple answer, I will give it in this manner without horns or teeth. Unless I am convicted by the testimony of Scripture or by clear reason (for I trust neither the pope nor councils alone, since it is well known that they have often erred and contradicted themselves), I am bound by the Scriptures I have cited, for my conscience is captive to the Word of God. 1 cannot and will not retract anything, since to act against one's conscience is neither safe nor right.* ***Here I stand I can do no other, so help me God?***[29]

A year later, after reflecting on this confrontation, Luther wrote the following:

> *I simply taught, preached and wrote Gods Word; otherwise, I did nothing. And then, while I slept or drank Wittenberg beer with my Philip and my Amsdorf, the Word greatly weakened the Papacy and never a Prince or Emperor inflicted such damage upon it. I did nothing. The Word did it all. Had I desired to cause trouble, I could have brought great bloodshed upon Germany. Yea, I could have started such a little game at Worms that the Emperor would not have been safe. But what would it have been?...I left it to the Word.*[30]

God's shield of protection was mighty around Luther. Many of the

27 John H. Leith, Creeds of the Churches, p. 451.

28 Ephesians 4:11-12

29 De Lamar, Confrontation at Worms, p. 52-56

30 C.M. Jacobs, trans., Works of Martin Luther, p. 99.

German electors were sympathetic to his case, particularly Frederick of Saxony and the Count Palatine; others feared political repercussions if they took too hostile a stand against this roaring professor. Franz von Sicicingen was ready to reduce Worms to rubble if Luther was harmed. "We have Franz on our side," wrote Ulrich von Hutten, "and he is not merely favorably disposed, but is red hot and burning."[31]

In the fury of papal thunder thrown against him, Luther's determination to publish his understandings was not hindered. In his writing, Against the Execrable Bull of Antichrist, Luther returns a fierce volley of defiance:

> *I ask thee, ignorant Antichrist, dost thou think that with thy naked words thou canst prevail against the armor of Scripture?...I can distinguish between inane [silly] paper and the omnipotent Word of God.*

After this surge of the Reformation, the Roman Catholic church was torn apart in western Europe. This changed the direction of the Church for all time.

The massive floodgates of reform had been opened. Not only would the European land mass be shaken, but across the Channel the effects would accelerate. In reference to English history, many secular historians believe that "the Constitutional cart came well before the spiritual horse."[32] I don't agree. Politics was not the only initial driving force; unknown to historians, it was Bible prophecy, "providence" that was the motivator! I see the English Reformation through the eyes of Scripture. I acknowledge that God can work through any means He desires, and has done so in order to fulfill His prophetic word. Is this a startling assertion? No, not if we understand the historical unfolding of the Book of Revelation, which was not silent concerning this most dramatic turning in the Christian Church. Briefly, let's examine the major events that occurred during the Reformation in England. Again, this will help our historical perspective.

The English Reformation occurred under King Henry VIII and his son, Edward VI. The same causes that Luther and the other reformers were espousing were present in England. Wycliffe had stirred the nation two centuries earlier, and his light was still shining.

Even though his Lollard followers had been crushed, the memory of this "Morning Star of the Reformation" had never been entirely forgotten. The ratio between these religious grievances and the national,

---

31 Johannes Janssen, History of the German People at the Close of the Middle Ages, p. 197-198.

32 Lacey Baldwin Smith, This Realm of England 1399 to 1688, p. 122.

political and economic motives is argued to this present day in academia. It was not till after the death of Henry VIII that England became, in the Christian sense, Protestant.

The story of Henry's needing a male heir to preserve the Tudor line is well known and can easily be researched. He would not wait on Rome, so in 1529 he called a Parliament which declared the English Church independent of Rome. By 1533 the English church was so far removed from the Roman Church that the Archbishop of Canterbury was able to grant the king his long-sought divorce.

The next year Parliament took the last step needed to establish the total independence of the English national church. All contacts with Rome were severed and Henry was declared by the "Act of Supremacy" to be absolute head of the Church of England. Therefore, this kingdom was severed from the once universal church. England was the first nation to break away from Rome's European spiritual city! This is a major fulfillment of a prophecy in the Book of Revelation. Let's turn there and see what John prophesied.

For centuries Protestant historicists have clearly understood that the tenth and eleventh chapters of the Book of Revelation foretold the glorious Reformation. In reference to the movement of applicable nations we read in Revelation 11:13a:

> *And the same hour was there a great earthquake, and the **tenth part** of the city fell, and in the earthquake were slain of men **seven thousand**...*

> The Book of Revelation was written in signs and symbols. It is a symbolic prophecy which must be translated into ordinary language before it can be understood. Let me here insert that it is my intention throughout this book to direct the reader to as many sources as possible. I will take the liberty of quoting them as often as deemed necessary. I am teaching nothing new. It is my burden to repair a terrible breech and restore foundationally straight paths.

Therefore, in reference to the symbolic nature of the Revelation, or of prophecy in general, I reference the words of Grattan Guinness (who many believe to have been England's greatest teacher of Bible prophecy):

> *It is clear that before a student can understand a given work, he must be acquainted with the language in which the book was written; and he must read it as written in that language, not in another. If the work be in French, he will fail to decipher its meaning if he reads the words as Latin or English.*

In what language is the Apocalypse written? Is it to be understood literally? If not, on what principle is it to be interpreted?

It is obvious to the most superficial reader, that in its actual texture and construction, the Apocalypse is a record of visions that are past. All allow, concerning its meaning, a prophecy of events that are future, or were future at the time that the visions were granted to St. John. The angel calls the book a prophecy, "seal not the sayings of the prophecy of this book, for the time is at hand." Of its prophetic character there can therefore be no more question, than that its form is a record of past visions. In the strictest sense, no one understands the book literally; for [example] the statement, "I saw a beast rise up out of the sea," taken literally, is in no sense whatever a prophecy; it is a narrative of a past event, not a prediction of a future one.

Such literalism as this is divinely excluded. John beheld things which were to take place "hereafter," but the future was signified to the apostle in a series of visions.

The book is "The Revelation of Jesus Christ, which God gave to Him, to show unto his servants things which must shortly come to pass; and He sent and signified it by his angel, unto his servant John."

To "signify" [semanio—signs and symbols] is to show by signs, to intimate your meaning, not in plain words, but by signs and symbols. [33]

In the visions of the Revelation, earthquakes are consistently interpreted to be great political upheavals. Certainly the Reformation was one the major earthquakes of all time. The effects of this earthquake, according to the vision, caused one tenth of a great city to fall away. In Revelation 17:18, Rome (as a spiritual empire) is identified as that great city. England was the first nation to tear herself away from the Holy Roman Empire after the prophetic earthquake of the Reformation. Through the leadership of Henry VIII, Edward VI, Queen Elizabeth and James the First, the British Monarchy became the head of the Church of England, not the pope. But is this too vague? Do we need more clarity? The remainder of verse 13, which states, "and in an earthquake were slain of men seven thousand," will help us pinpoint this epic turmoil in Reformation Europe. To do this, we must look at the events which led up to the revolt of the Netherlands.

The Holy Roman Emperor Charles V had a son named Philip II (1556-98). Philip is noted in history as Spain's "Most Catholic King." This king's reign is referred to as the "Golden Age of Spain." During

33 H. Grattan Guinness, The Approaching End of the Age, p. 99- 100.

the time of Philip, Spain was the nerve center of the Catholic Reformation. Also, by the time of Philip, the Spanish Inquisition had reached its apex. The Inquisition in Spain was established in 1487 by Ferdinand and Isabella, and first headed by the notorious Thomas de Torquemada. It was independent of the medieval Inquisition and was controlled by the Spanish kings. It was far better organized, harsher and freer with the death sentence than its counterpart. Its attempted introduction into the Netherlands led to rebellion.

The Netherlands then consisted of seventeen provinces. The humanism of Erasmus as well as the teachings of Luther took early root in the nation, soon to be followed by Anabaptist ideas. But in the 1550s a militant, disciplined Calvinism spread rapidly and soon became the dominant form of Protestantism. The revolt was tripart in nature. First, there was a reaction against centralization. Secondly, a patriotic fervor surfaced, and thirdly, there was a religious protest against inquisitorial Catholicism.

The year 1566 marked a drastic acceleration of the revolt. Calvinist mobs began to break images of the saints and smashed the stained glass windows in Catholic churches throughout the seventeen provinces. Philip reacted by sending in the Duke of Alva with ten thousand troops. Alva instituted what came to be known as "the Council of Blood." He boasted that he had executed over seventeen thousand people. This council lasted for six years, and the people of the Netherlands never forgot this hellish scourge. In 1576, Antwerp was sacked by Spanish troops in what is known as the "Spanish Fury." All seventeen provinces were frightened into submission and agreed to stay together with the Pacification of Ghent.

Within three years, all moderation lost influence. The majority of Catholics looked to Spain for protection. The seventeen provinces divided. The Calvinists fled to the Dutch provinces of the north, beyond the great rivers where they were able to set up adequate defenses. The Catholics went south to the Walloon provinces. In 1579 the seven Dutch provinces in the north formed the Union of Utrecht. It was the foundation of the United Provinces or Dutch Netherlands. They formally declared their independence from Spain in 1581. The prophetic Word of God was fulfilled, "and in an earthquake were slain of men seven thousand" (Rev. 11:13).

All in the futurist school, and many in the historicist school, have wrestled with the interpretation of this verse. However, I reference Horae Apocalypticae (part III, pages 457-467). Here, Elliott interprets this verse with unmatched scholastic genius. He proves that the word "thousands" is properly interpreted chiliads, meaning provinces or counties. It is important to see how simply and beautifully history falls into proper perspective with this enlightenment.

Thus, we look for seven chiliads of the papal city to break away about the time England (one tenth of the city) rebels. You have already read the history of this fulfillment. The Union of Utrecht formed these seven chiliads that fell away. These are the seven provinces ("thousands," KJV) that fell away as a result of the Reformation: Holland, Zealand, Utrecht, Freiseland, Groningen, Overyssel and Guiderland. The Revelation is no mystery. It is a revelation!

The sixteenth century was a fierce blow to Rome's temporal and spiritual authority. Her doctrines crumbled before the teachings of the reformers and nations were beginning to leave her empire of superstition. However, history bears witness that she was not about to have her voice silenced. Rome moved forcefully and swiftly into her Counter-Reformation. The Council of Trent, 1546, rejected all the fundamental claims of the reformers:

Reformation:	***Council of Trent:***
Sola Scriptura (Scriptures only)	Tradition equals Scripture
Christ sacrificed once	Christ's sacrifice is perpetuated in the mass
Salvation by faith	Salvation by works

At the time of this doctrinal struggle, all Bible-believing Protestants believed that the seventy weeks (490 day-years) of Daniel nine had run their prophetic course in entirety. As a matter of fact, this was also taught by the Catholic church. Not one Protestant would have thought of separating the time measure with two thousand years of Church history. The idea of putting antichrist exclusively at the end of the age was not even considered. Nevertheless, this is exactly what Rome did. In Part II of this book we'll examine the origin of futuristic teaching, and how these teachings merged into Protestant theology. We'll discover who first taught this form of eschatology, and who was the first Protestant scholar to acquiesce to these interpretations. Futurism was formulated in the heat of Reformation and Counter-Reformation fury. It is designed for one purpose only: safeguarding the papacy from the scathing attacks of the Protestants!

Part Two
Tracing the Infusion of Error

The Jesuits

The Jesuits are a religious order of the Roman Catholic church. Their proper title is the "Society of Jesus." Originally they were called Compania de Jestis, which is Spanish for "(military) company of Jesus." They were founded (1534-39) by Ignatius of Loyola. He drafted the rules that still govern the society. The training of a Jesuit is long and rigorous. Though not often taught, they were basically founded to combat the Reformation. Jesuit leaders played a major role in Rome's Counter-Reformation. In the 16th and 17th century, this corps labored with measured success in reconverting Protestant areas in South and West Germany, Hungary, France and Poland. They also made several aggressive attempts to reconvert England.

The Christian Church is basically unaware that the futurist school came from this society's scholars. Jesuit priests have been known throughout history as the most wicked political arm of the Roman Catholic church. Edmond Paris, in his scholarly work, The Secret History of the Jesuits, reveals and documents much of this information. Their political intrigue has caused them to be banned from several nations throughout the course of their dubious history. Here is a brief list of nations, and provinces with the dates they expelled the Jesuit order: Portugal 1759, France 1764, Spain 1767, Naples 1767, Parma and Russia 1820. Several of these nations have once again allowed them entrance. The popes themselves know how wicked this order is. There is much evidence to implicate them in the death of Pope Clement XIV, who was poisoned in 1773.[34]

In 1585, a Jesuit priest named Francisco Ribera (1537-1591) started to work independently. He looked deeply into the realm of Bible prophecy. The result of his work was a twisting and maligning of prophetic truth. Ribera's futuristic interpretation of Daniel chapter nine was furthered by the work of another Jesuit, Cardinal Robert Bellarmine (1542-1621). These two were swiftly followed by a third, the Jesuit Luis de Alcazar (1554-1613). These men were the best soldiers Rome had. No one ever said Rome wasn't smart. Consistently, when she wants something done, she commissions her best men. Lord, help the Protestants to understand this effective principle. Let us quit raising up men who just agree with everybody. Instead, give us men of courage, truth and wisdom, scholars who are passionately driven by the anointing of the Holy Spirit. Let's

34 William Cathcart, The Papal System, p. 462-464.

identify the areas of deception for which these papal warriors were responsible.

In exposing the Romish apocalyptic expositors of the Reformation era, Elliott has given a synopsis of their prophetic positions:

> *So at length, as the century [16th] was advancing to a close, two stout Jesuits took up the gauntlet; and published their respective, but quite counter opinions on the Apocalyptic subject:—the one **Ribera**, a Jesuit Priest of Salamanca, who about A.D. 1585 published an Apocalyptic Commentary, which was on the grand points of Babylon and Antichrist what we now call the futurist scheme: the other, Alcazar, also a Spanish Jesuit, but of Seville, whose scheme was on main points what we now designate as that of the **praeterists**.*[35]

In taking up the gauntlet, these men could not have imagined that their works would be primarily taught by Protestants in the 20th century! For over three hundred years futurism and praeterism (which we shall define later) were rejected by the majority of ministers as deceptive hermeneutics from the Roman Catholic church. Now, futurism reigns triumphant, and praeterism is claiming to be the true alternative. God help us! It's time to dismantle this reign of prophetic chaos by clearly exposing the authors and their intent, and by establishing the truth which will scatter all contenders.

When Ribera's commentary first appeared in England, it "excited vehemently the indignation" of the Protestants. The English expositor Brightman read the work and defiantly countered in his Commentary:

> *But mine anger and indignation burst out against the Jesuits. For when as I had by chance light upon Ribera, who had made a Commentary upon the same holy Revelation, Is it even so? said I. Do the Papist take heart again; so as that book, which of long time before they would scarce suffer any man to touch, they dare now take in hand, to intreat fully upon it? What! was it but a vain image or bug, at the sight whereof they were wont to tremble a few years since, even in the dim light, that now they dare behold to look wishly upon this glasse in the clear sunshine and dare proclaime to the world that any other thing rather is poynted [pointed] at in it than their Pope of Rome?*[36]

In his excellent book, ***Great Prophecies of the Bible***, Ralph Woodrow summarized the prophetic doctrine of Ribera:

---

35 Horae Apocalypticae, "History of Apocalyptic Interpretation," p. 465.

36 Ibid. p. 465-466.

Ribera published a 500-page commentary on the grand points of Babylon and Antichrist an Sacram Beati Ionnis Apostoli & Evangelistate Apocoalypsin Commentart, (Lugduni, 1593). The object being to set aside the Protestant teachings that the Papacy is the antichrist. [Ribera's writings are still found in the Bodleian Library, Oxford, England.] In his commentary, he assigns the first chapters of Revelation to the first century. The rest he restricted to a literal three and a half years at the end of time. He taught that the Jewish temple would be rebuilt by a single individual antichrist who would abolish the Christian religion, deny Christ, pretend to be God, and conquer the world.[37]

Does this sound familiar? Have we heard these scenarios all too often taught in Protestant churches? Did any of your teachers ever tell you who authored them? Even secular historians record the tactics of Counter-Reformation Rome. The Encyclopedia Britannica states, "Under the stress of the Protestant attack there arose new methods on the papal side."[38] Ribera is identified as the founder of the futurist school of interpretation.

William E. Biederwolf, in his Bible commentary, comes to the following conclusion as to the origin of the futurist system:

This school was launched in 1580 [1585] by the Jesuit Ribera, who, as Guinness says, "moved like Alcazar to relieve the Papacy from the terrible stigma cast upon it by the Protestant interpretation (the Historical School), tried to do so by referring these prophecies to the distant future, instead of like Alcazar to the distant past."[39]

While editing Jonathan Edwards' ***Apocalyptic Writings***, Stephen J. Stein commented:[40]

The polemical bent of Protestant exegetes produced an inevitable response from the Roman Catholic community. Near the turn of the seventeenth century two prominent Jesuits wrote commentaries offering different interpretations of the Revelation. Francisco Ribera contended that the prophecies of the Antichrist were still unfulfilled. The Antichrist was to be a Jewish deceiver of the world who would reign for three and a half years. By contrast, Luis de Alcasar thought that the prophecies of the Apocalypse had already been fulfilled in

37 Ralph Woodrow, Great Prophecies of the Bible, p. 196-197.

38 Encyclopedia Britannica, vol. 23, p. 213. 11th edition.

39 William E. Biederwolf, The Second Coming Bible Commentary, p. 569.

40 Jonathan Edwards, Apocalyptic Writings, Stephen J. Stein, Ed., "Editor's Introduction," pp. 3-4.

the struggles of the early Church with Judaism and paganism. The last two chapters of the Revelation, he said, tell of the triumph of the Roman Catholic Church.

I will emphasize a fundamental truth once more; the futurist school of Bible prophecy was created for one reason, and one reason only: to counter the Protestant Reformation!

Ribera's primary apparatus was the seventy weeks. He taught that Daniel's 70th week was still in the future. He said that God had first given us 69 weeks and that at the baptism of Jesus in 27 A.D. the 69 weeks concluded. He said that God extended the 70th week into the future to take place at the end of the age. It was as though God put a giant rubber band on this Messianic time measure. Does this supposition sound familiar? This is exactly the scenario used by Hal Lindsey and a multitude of other current prophecy teachers.

Remember, Ribera was not alone in his efforts to war on the Protestant cause. Cardinal Robert Bellarmine eagerly accepted the challenge and entered into the arena. Woodrow presents a relevant biography of this man's contribution to the confusion:

The futurist teachings of Ribera were further popularized by an Italian cardinal and the most renowned of all Jesuit controversialists. His writings claimed that Paul, Daniel and John had nothing whatsoever to say about the Papal power. The futurists' school won general acceptance among Catholics. They were taught that antichrist was a single individual who would not rule until the very end of time. But this effort to sidetrack the teachings that the Papacy is the antichrist failed to hold back the advancing tide of Protestant truth—at least for a while.[41]

Let me add that Bellarmine followed very closely the teachings of Ribera. However, Ribera only partially attacked the year-for-a-day principle, whereas Bellarmine declared absolute war against it. The systematic theology of interpreting Divine time measures a day for a year, when the text dictates, has been almost entirely lost to the Protestant church. However, the hypocrisy of the matter is manifest continually in the futurist school. They are forced to acknowledge this principle of interpretation with the seventy weeks, but with other Divine time measures (i.e., the Book of Revelation) they reject this great principle and try to teach that they are to be interpreted as literal days! By what authority do they do this? Ribera's, not God's!

---

41 Great Prophecies of the Bible, p. 198.

The Bible has several Divine time measures incorporated in the prophetic utterances. Why aren't these time measures broken and separated from their contexts? ***"...the scripture cannot be broken;" John 10:35***. Why do the futurists only take this liberty with the seventy weeks? I hope by now you are beginning to understand why. It's an infusion of error that futurist teachers can't explain. Why do they try to tell us that God broke the seventy weeks? We must examine this if we are to be honest with ourselves and God. I will substantiate that God never broke this great prophecy; man altered it in his mind. Satan would deceive us all and rob us of our understanding of destiny!

The breaking of the seventy weeks is the cracked foundation stone for futurism and dispensationalism. These interpretations must have their seven-year period at the end of time. Remember, this is the last week of the 490-year prophetic clock. All futurist scenarios revolve around Ribera's "seven-year tribulation period." This erroneous presumption will be shattered as we proceed. Truth will triumph!

It is systematic teaching that will usher in the return to the true historical interpretation and fulfillment of the vision. (The implications of this will be self-evident and discussed in relation to the Kingdom and the restoration of truth within its walls.) The proper date and decree that signaled the start of the time measure must be established. The seventy weeks began in 457 B.C., and conclude, in entirety, in 34 A.D. God's Word gives us an unmistakably clear signal as to when this period was to initiate and to culminate. The apostles knew they were to restrict their movements until that time span ran its course. This was necessary because of its exclusive application to the Jews. Further, it will be seen that the stoning of Stephen was not the end of this measure; God gave us a much more accurate indication.

However, on the other end of the prophetic spectrum, our third Jesuit must be addressed. Luis de Alcazar attempted to divert the Protestant attacks by pointing fifteen centuries into the past and planting antichrist there.

Alcazar wrote on the Ribera school of thought. His book was entitled, Vestigatio Arcani Senses in Apocalypsi, published in Antwerp, 1614. He launched the praeterist (often spelled "preterist") school of apocalyptic interpretation. The preterists consider the majority of the prophecies in the Book of Revelation to have been fulfilled in the downfall of the Jewish nation in 70 A.D. Most advocates of this system date John's writing of the Revelation prior to 68 A.D. Nero, they claim, was the Antichrist. This interpretation, in my opinion, is easily discredited. The preterists find themselves in the same contradictions as the futurists. The systematic theology of the year-day principle in Bible prophecy thwarts their schemes. By what authority do preterists say that Revelation's divine time measures are interpreted a day for a day? Like the entirety of the futurist camp, they turn around and say that the seventy weeks are to be interpreted as years. An immense contradiction!

Alcazar's main thrust, like that of Ribera and Bellarmine before him, was to protect the papacy. His admiration for the "Vicar of Christ" is clearly stated:

> *That Rome of old, head of Pagan idolatry, by an admirable vicissitude [change of circumstances] was to be changed into the metropolis of the Catholic Church; that the Roman Church was gloriously to triumph both in respect of the Roman city and the whole empire; and that the sovereign authority of the Romish Pope should always remain in the height of honour.*[42]

Elliott sharply rebuked the preterist teaching by referencing the understanding of Irenaeus, the grand pupil of the Apostle John:

> *On the contrary, the early testimony of Irenaeus, disciple to Polycarp, who was himself a disciple to St. John, indicates a then totally different view of the Apocalyptic Beast...As if the only one ever known to have been received: a view referring it, not to any previous persecution by Nero and the Roman Empire under him, but to an Antichrist even then future; one that was to arise and persecute the church NOT till the breaking up, and reconstruction in another form, of the old Empire.*[43]

Alcazar's Antichrist ....Church Age.................Ribera's Antichrist

PAST ***?*** ***FUTURE***

In concluding the Jesuit infusion, Ecclesiastes warns us in a proverb that, "a threefold cord is not quickly broken."[44] The threefold cord of the Jesuit writers has done its damage. The extent of confusion is almost unbelievable. I have often wondered how such great Protestant ministers could be so deceived. That question is left to the judgments of the heart—God's realm. The fruit, however, is what we must test. Thankfully, the historical chronology of Protestant responsibility is traceable and verifiable. It begins in 1826, with a man named Samuel Roffey Maitland.

---

42 Horae Apocalypticae, APP. Part I., p. 468.

43 Ibid, Appendix Section II. "German Neronic Preterist Counter-scheme."

44 Ecclesiates 4:12

The Protestants

S.R. Maitland (1792-1866) was the librarian to the Archbishop of Canterbury. He was appointed by Archbishop William Howdy, Keeper of the Manuscripts at Lambeth Palace, London, where the massive library of the Church of England was kept.

> *It was then that Dr. Maitland discovered this futurist view of the Revelation, as taught by Francisco Ribera from Spain, and he published it just for the sake of interest.*[45]

These events began in 1826. At this time the vast majority of American Protestants were historicists. It is understood that Maitland had much contempt for the Reformation, and he did not believe that the papacy was the predicted antichristian Apostasy or Beast of Daniel and the apocalypse. I challenge you to find one Protestant who believed the futuristic teachings of the seventy weeks before 1826. It is impossible!

Dr. Maitland wrote a prophetic pamphlet in which he challenged the generally understood year-day view of the 1260 days of Daniel and the Revelation. This was in 1826. In 1829 and 1830, a Second Inquiry into the same subjects appeared. To make things worse, in 1833 the "Oxford Tracts" were published, whose chief object was to deprotestantize the Church of England! Error was now tumbling into the Protestant theological mainstream. A consuming virus had set in, and it will take its toll for decades to come.

In 1851, the brilliant Elliott published the fourth edition of the Horae Apocalypticae. In this massive work, he refutes the most intellectual and witty counter-schemes, several which have already been mentioned. However, his main concern was the damage already being done by Dr. Maitland. He addresses this concern in the Preface to the fourth edition:

> *At the time when the author's thoughts were first seriously directed to the study of Prophecy, the Rev. S.R. Maitland's publications had begun to make an evident impression on English theological students, more especially such as were investigators of prophecy; and had caused doubt in the minds of many, not only as to the correctness of the old Protestant anti-Romish views of the Apocalypse, and of the prophetic year-day theory therewith essentially connected, but doubt whether the apocalypse had as yet received any fulfillment in the past history of the Church and Christendom.*

---

45 Thomas Foster, The Pope, Communism and the Coming New World, p. 2.

Maitland's errors were magnified by John Nelson Darby (1800- 1882). Darby read the pamphlets that Maitland produced and was persuaded. This man was the founder of the Plymouth Brethren. He thought this was a great revelation—with such a simplified view of Bible prophecy, there was no need to understand the historic application. It was all in the future! Darby wrote several volumes on this new understanding of prophecy. He influenced many people, including Cyrus Ingerson Scofield (1843-1921). To make things worse, Darby's views were incorporated in the Scofield Reference Bible, 1909.

Darby in turn was followed by William Kelly. This relationship, which included many others, is summarized by Alexander Reese in his unmatched scholarly refutation of the pretribulation rapture teaching (the rapture theory will be discussed later) entitled The Approaching Advent of Christ:

> *About 1830...a new school arose within the fold of Premillennialism that sought to overthrow what, since the Apostolic Age, had been considered by all premillenialists as established results, and to institute in their place a series of doctrines that had never been heard before. The school I refer to is that of "The Brethren" or "Plymouth Brethren," founded by J.N. Darby.*
>
> *It will be convenient to give a summary of the new doctrines, with extracts from writings of the four pioneer writers who filled Evangelical Christendom with their teachings. I refer to Darby's Lectures on the Second Coming and Notes on the Apocalypse, Kelly's Lectures on the Second Coming and Kingdom of the Lord Jesus Christ, Christ's Coming Again, and Lectures on the Book of Revelation, Molter 's Plain Papers on Prophetic Subjects, and C.H.M.'s Papers on the Lord's Coming.*
>
> *In America the new teachings were spread abroad through W.E. Blackstone 's Jesus Is Coming, and numerous writings of F. W. Grant, J.M. Gray, A.C. Gaebelein, F.C. Ottman and C.I. Scofield, but all these followed the lead of the British (or Irish) pioneers. Scofield's Reference Bible represents a lifelong study of the Scriptures, and is hailed in all the world by Brethren as setting forth their views on the interpretation of Scripture, especially of prophecy and "dispensational truth." And naturally: Scofield was for a generation an assiduous and admiring student of Darby's writings. In A.C. Gaebelein's many writings the influence and spirit of William Kelly are everywhere evident...*[46]

46 Alexander Reese, The Approaching Advent of Christ, p. 19.

Today, the ripple effect of these men's teachings fills the Christian bookstores. I am not attacking their great Christian lives, only that which they wrote on eschatology. Fortunately, many students of Bible prophecy are turning away from the futurist school of interpretation. It is to be hoped that they will not be deceived by the new wave of preterist teachers. Theirs is not the true alternative. The erroneous futurist predictions during the decade of the 1980s have left many people confused and disappointed with prophecy teachers. God's people are once again recognizing the providential hand of the Lord upon them. They are refusing to endure teachings which are confusing and contradicting.

I hope this brief chronology will encourage you to question the roots of many prophetic teachings you have heard over the years. Remember, if the root is bad, how much more rotten the fruit will be! Don't let men keep you from being a Berean.

Part Three
Historicism: Five Relevant Teachings

The Little Horn

In Daniel seven, there is an account of a remarkable prophetic dream which Daniel had in the first year of the reign of Belshazzar. Likewise, this prophet is given the interpretation. Let us examine this startling vision. I shall quote in a partly abridged version from verses 1 through 8.

1. *In the first year of Belshazzar, king of Babylon, Daniel had a dream...he wrote the dream, and told the sum of the matters.*
2. *Daniel spake and said, I saw...four winds of heaven strove upon the great sea.*
3. *And FOUR GREAT BEASTS came up from the sea, different one from another.*
4. *The first was like a LION, AND HAD EAGLE'S WINGS.*
5. *And behold another beast, a second, LIKE TO A BEAR, and it raised itself on one side, and it had THREE RIBS in the mouth of it, between the teeth of it.*
6. *After this I beheld, and to another, LIKE A LEAPORD, which had upon the back of it FOUR WINGS OF A FOWL; the breast had also FOUR HEADS; and dominion was given to it.*
7. *After this I saw in the night visions, and beheld a FOURTH BEAST, dreadful and terrible, and strong exceedingly...and IT HAD TEN HORNS.*
8. *I considered the horns, and, behold, there came up among them another LITTLE HORN, before whom there were THREE of the first horns plucked up...*

An outline of the true historical interpretation will help to orient you as you read part of the vision's fulfillment.

DANIEL 7:3-8

v.4 BABYLON

v.5 MEDO-PERSIA

The three ribs:	Babylon
	Egypt
	Lydia

v.6 GREECE

The four heads:	Cassander—ruled Greece	
	Lysimachus—ruled Asia Minor	
	Seleucus—ruled Syria and Babylon	
	Ptolemy—ruled Egypt	

v.7 ROME (Pagan)

v.8 GOTHIC NATION (West)

The ten horns:	Vandals	Heruli
	Suevi	Franks
	Visigoths	Allemani
	Ostragoths	Huns
	Lombards	Burgundians

v.8 LITTLE HORN (Papacy)

The three plucked up:	Lombards
	Vandals
	Ostrogothe

THE FOUR BEASTS

BABYLON

The first of these four great beasts was "like a lion, and had eagle wings." In this vision in Daniel seven the empire which had been represented by the most costly and precious of metals in Daniel two was now represented by the king of beasts with the wings of the king of birds. The vision was fulfilled in the ancient Babylonian Empire and its magnificent capital city, Babylon, whose splendor has become legendary.

This empire of golden grandeur and lion's strength is referred to in Isaiah 13:19 as "the glory of kingdoms, the beauty of the Chaldees' excellency." Isaiah 14:4 calls it "the golden city." ("Thou art this head of gold," Dan. 2:38.) And Jeremiah describes it as "the praise of the whole earth" (Jer. 51:41).

MEDO-PERSIA

The Persian Empire was represented in Daniel two by the great image's breast and arms of silver. In chapter seven the imagery of a bear, rising up on one side (until this point it had been at rest) and with three ribs in its mouth is used to represent the same empire.

In 550 B.C. the Persian, Cyrus, captured Ecbatane, capital of the kingdom of Media, and deposed Astyages their king. He amalgamated Media with the Persian kingdom, hence the rise of the Medo-Persian empire.

Croesus, king of Lydia, whose name is still proverbially linked with great riches, attacked the Persians. But he was smashed by Cyrus, who in turn took Sardis, his capitol.

Cyrus then attacked Nabonidus and the main Babylonian army. Having successfully routed them, he marched on the city of Babylon itself and captured it. His son Cambyses conquered Egypt. The three ribs in the mouth of the bear represent Lydia, Babylon and Egypt.

The conquest of Egypt by the Persians was further established by Darius I (521-486 B.C.), then completed by Xerxes (486-467 B.C.).

GREECE

In Daniel seven the ancient Greek Empire is likened to a leopard with four heads and four wings. This is perfect symbolism for the rise and later four-fold subdivision of the great Grecian empire with its military genius, Alexander the Great.

The leopard is a very swift animal, and this was an important fact of Alexander the Great's tactics in the military prowess and conquests which built his empire.

The wings on the leopard also represent his swiftness and agility of military maneuver; and the four heads represent the four subdivisions of his empire after his death (Cassander, Lysimachus, Selucus and Ptolemy). Darius III was conquered by Alexander at the three battles of Grancius, Issus and Guagamela. He had a dream of forging Europe and Asia together into a single political, cultural and, possibly, linguistic unit. He died before this dream could be fulfilled.

ROME

Daniel seven prophesied that the fourth successive empire (Roman) would be "dreadful and terrible, and strong exceedingly; and it had great iron teeth; it devoured and brake in pieces, and stamped from the residue with the feet of it: and it was diverse from all the beasts that were before it; and it had ten horns."

This is the predicted rise of the ancient Roman Empire which succeeded the Greek and existed from B.C. into A.D. During its reign of conquest, our Lord and Savior Jesus Christ lived and died for the sins of the world. And during the era of the Roman Empire the New Testament canon was completed.

When one reads Edward Gibbons' Decline and Fall of the Roman Empire, it becomes clear that as the Romans deteriorated morally, their empire started to come apart at the seams until the fifth century A.D. It was only a matter of time until the whole structure, especially the western half of the Empire, simply fell to pieces in the face of the militaristic incursions of what the Romans called "barbarian hordes."

In 410 AD., the then reigning Emperor, Honorius, recalled all his legions from Britannia back to Europe to help defend their European frontiers. Hence Britain was evacuated lock, stock and barrel by the Romans in 410 A.D. under Honorius' decree.

This only helped stave off final disaster until 476 A.D. In that tumultuous year, Romulus Augustulus, the last western Roman Emperor, was deposed by Odacer, the leader of the Heruli. In fulfillment of Daniel chapters two and seven, the western Empire began its subdivision into ten different kingdoms (Vandals, Suevi, Visigoths, Ostrogoths, Heruli, Franks, Allemani, Huns, Lombards and Burgundians). Daniel had predicted that these ten "toes" or "horns" would "not cleave one to another." Historically, this was precisely fulfilled. Instead, they cleaved to papal ideology.

Britannia is also included by most scholars, but from a historical perspective we do well to remember that under the decree of Honorius, Britain was totally evacuated. This took place 66 years, at least a generation, before Romulus Augustulus was deposed. Britain was also invaded by the Anglo-Saxons before 476 AD.[47]

We have now seen prophecy and history bring us to the point of the "little horn" of Daniel 7:8,24.

> *v.8 I considered the horns, and, behold, there came up among them another little horn, before whom there were three of the first horns plucked up…*

> *v.24 And the ten horns out of this kingdom are ten kings that shall arise: and another shall rise after them; and he shall be diverse from the first, and he shall subdue three kings.*

All that is needed is a look back in history to see if this prophecy was exactly fulfilled. If it was not fulfilled, then it is, as the futurists say, "yet to come." Can we identify three of the horns (nations) which struggled against, and were plucked up by, the infamous little horn?

47 The information of the Beast was extracted from the late Rev. David Campbell's book, Signs Are for Strangers, pp. 33-39. If it were not for David, I would be of men most miserable in my search for prophetic truth!

Yes, we can! This is not a future occurrence. Neither is it a complicated matter of research This event perfectly unfolded in unbroken historical chronology.

In the year 533 A.D. the horn of the Vandals in Africa, Corsica and Sardinia, and shortly after, that of the Ostrogoths in Italy was rooted up by Justinian's forces under Belisarius. The Lombard horn was eradicated by Pepin and Charlemagne.

By the year 752 A.D. the three horns which posed a threat to the rise of the "little horn" (the Bishop of Rome, or the emerging papacy) were completely plucked up by the roots. Exactly as predicted, this great prophecy was fulfilled! Why do we let the futurists throw this into the future and tell us the little horn is yet to come? This is what Ribera taught. It's exactly what Rome wants the Protestants to believe. The Reformation fathers knew better.

The diversity of this little horn was seen by Daniel. It would claim not only temporal, but spiritual domination as well. We also know that it was unmistakenly to be a Roman power. The fourth beast of Daniel seven was Rome. It was to emerge preeminent among ten new kingdoms. The exact identity was enhanced with the prediction that it would defeat three kingdoms (horns) that resisted its rise. It would also "speak great words against the Most High." Libraries are filled with texts documenting these "great words" of contempt for true Bible Christianity. I believe Guinness correctly identified this apostasy:

> *Is not the Papacy sufficiently diverse from all the rest of the kingdoms of western Europe to identify it as the little horn? What other ruling monarch of Christendom ever pretended to apostolic authority, or ruled men in the name of God? Does the pope dress in royal robes? Nay, but in priestly garments. Does he wear a crown? Nay, but a triple tiara, to show that he reigns in heaven, earth, and hell! Does he wield a sceptre? Nay, but a crosier or crook, to show that he is the good shepherd of the Church. Do his subjects kiss his hand? Nay, but his toe! Verily this power is "diverse" from the rest, both in great things and in little. It is small in size, gigantic in its pretensions.*[48]

In conclusion, Daniel said that this terrible little horn would make "war with the saints," and prevail against them. Is Daniel saying that the saints of God will have to face this oppression and patiently endure it? Yes he is, and yes they did. For thirteen centuries God's saints were "worn out" by the one "whose look was more stout than his fellows." "It has been calculated that the Popes of Rome have, directly or indirectly,

48 H. Grattan Guinness' Romanism and the Reformation, p. 28.

slain on account of their faith, fifty millions of martyrs!"[49] God has not forgotten!

49 Ibid, p. 212.

Seven Kings

Revelation 17:8-11:

v.8 The beast that thou sawest was, and is not; and shall ascend out of the bottomless pit, and go into perdition: and they that dwell on the earth shall wonder, whose names were not written in the book of life from the foundation of the world, when they behold the beast that was, and is not, and yet is.

v.9 And here is the mind which hath wisdom. The seven heads are seven mountains [Palatine, Quirinal, Aventine, Caelian, Viminal, Esquiline and the Janiculan], on which the woman sitteth. [Strong indicates that the Greek word used here for mountain is oros and that it means "a mountain (as lifting itself above the plain), hill, mount[ain]."]

v.10 And there are seven kings [basileus—foundations of power]: five are fallen, and one is, and the other is not yet come; and when he cometh, he must continue a short space.

v.11 And the beast that was, and is not, even he is eight, and is of the seven, and goeth into perdition.

The Apostle John is given a great revelation as to the identity of the "beast, that was and is not, and yet is." In the Book of Revelation, this is the third appearance of the ten-horned beast. Historically, it first appeared as Rome Pagan, then transitioned into Rome Papal. Its third appearance is for our time, manifesting itself in the European Economic Community (EEC), embracing a socialist mentality.

John tells us that we must look toward the "seven hilled city" to properly recognize this beast. This city could only be Rome.

In St. John's time Rome was called (as it is to this very day) "the seven hilled city." I have already identified the historic names of the seven hills The seven-hilled city of Rome also had an annual national festival called Septimontiun, "The Festival of Seven Mountains."

On the coins and Imperial Medals of John's day, which are located in various museums, we find Rome proudly displayed as a woman sitting on seven hills, the unchallenged matron of the world as it was then, even as she is represented in the Book of Revelation.

This "BABYLON" of Revelation was still in the future in John's day and although it would be located in the seven hilled city it was to be different from the Pagan empire. In fact it would be spiritual. Cardinal Bellarmine was one of Rome's greatest thinkers and controversialists, and he declared, "John, in the Apocalypse [i.e., the Book of Revelation] calls Rome, Babylon." Another great Roman writer, Cardinal Baronius, said, "Rome is signified by Babylon; it is confessed of all" Bishop Bossuet, another of their thinkers, said, "All the Fathers taught that the Babylon of the Apocalypse is Rome." In like manner Bishop Walmsley, Alcazar and numerous other Roman Catholic theologians have admitted the same.[50]

In order to answer this perplexity (actually, it's a revelation), we must look at the history of Rome. It is not well known that she had seven forms of government (or foundations of power) before the eighth appeared. In his great work, The Approaching End of the Age, p. 162, H. Grattan Guinness identified these distinct forms of sovereignty:

The great Roman power did actually exist under seven distinct... forms of government, enumerated by Livy, Tacitus, and historians in general, as such. Rome was ruled successively by KINGS, CONSULS, DICTATORS, DECEMVIRS, MILITARY TRIBUNES, MILITARY EMPERORS [Caesars], AND DESPOTIC EMPERORS, [emphasis added].

Guinness went on to say on page 170:

Seven kings formed the first head, and lasted 220 years; consuls, tribunes, decemvirs [a council of ten magistrates which lasted from 451-449 and drew up the law code of the Twelve Tables], and dictators, were the next four heads, and governed Rome in turn for nearly 500 years; sixty-five emperors [caesars] followed, and ruled the Roman world for 500 years more. Now the man of sin, Antichrist, is to be the last, and the most important "head" of this same Roman beast.

We must remember that John wrote the Revelation during the time of the caesars. The prophecy stated, "five are fallen." The kings, consuls, dictators, decemvirs, and military tribunals had all passed away (fallen). "And one is," the sixth or present form, the caesars. "And the other is not yet come." These were the emperors, the seventh form.

John said that after the first seven forms of government passed away, another (the eighth) would arise and go into perdition. After the last emperor was toppled in 476 A.D., the eighth form of Roman government, the papacy, ascended into power. Who dares deny that it was "of the seven" before it? Does the pope, to this very day, claim the title

---

50 David Campbell, Signs are for Strangers, p. 42.

Pontifex Maximus, which was held by all the Roman Emperors? Simple to understand, isn't it? This is no mystery, it's a revelation!

For centuries, Protestants have believed what has been presented to you here. Can you begin to understand what has happened to the seventy weeks? If people will believe that the final week (seven years) of Daniel's prophecy is yet to occur, and that the seals, trumpets and vials of the Book of Revelation are restricted to this time frame (instead of progressively unfolding during the Church Age), then the greatest witness against the apostate church in the Word of God is destroyed. I read clearly in the Revelation that John was told: "Seal not the sayings of the prophecy of this book: for the time is at hand."[51]

Let's tie these two great prophecies together with the teachings of the apostle Paul in his second letter to the Thessalonians; thus we further expose the fabrication of the dispensationalists.

51 Revelation 22:10

The Hindrance

Second Thessalonians 2:5-7

v.5 Remember ye not, that, when I was yet with you, I told you these things?

v.6 And now ye know what withholdeth that he [the man of sin] might be revealed in his time.

v.7 ...only he who letteth [hinders] will let, until he be taken out of the way.

The word "letteth" (let) can properly be interpreted "restrain." What was the hindrance to the emergence of the Man of Sin, i.e., the Little Horn, or the eighth form of Roman government? In the primary case, the apostle speaks of it in the neuter gender—"you know WHAT withholds." Then he uses the masculine gender—"HE who now hinders." The only logical conclusion is that the hindrance or restrainer will be both neuter and masculine. As long as the Roman Empire was under pagan rule, the Man of Sin could not take his place of authority in the seven-hilled city. Thus the "hindrance" in the primary neuter gender is fulfilled in the Roman Empire, and the same "hindrance" in the masculine gender was fulfilled in the despotic emperors. They had to be taken out of the way first. We have already seen how this happened with the Gothic invasions. In 476 A.D., Rome Pagan vanished in the west, only to be replaced by apostate Rome Papal. It was like one rising from the dead, surviving a mortal head wound! (See Revelation 13:3.) The following is a brief list of statements confirming this understanding:

Chrysostom, Bishop of Constantinople, 390 A.D., writes, "By the 'Hindrance' Paul means the Roman Empire." This was also believed by Augustine, Bishop of Hippo, 400 A.D.

Jerome, 400 A.D., declared, "If St. Paul had written openly and boldly that the man of sin would not come until the Roman Empire was destroyed, a just cause of persecution would then appear to have been afforded against the Church in her infancy."

Bishop Wodsworth wrote in 1850, "The earliest Christian writers declare...with one voice the 'he who letteth' was the heathen Roman Empire." (Apocalypse, p. 520)

The Amplified Bible, 1958 footnote of Second Thessalonians 2:6 states, "Many believe this one who restrains the Antichrist to be the Holy

Spirit…A majority think it refers to the Roman Empire."

This has been the consistent voice of the historicist school for century after century. On the other hand, the futurist view was cleverly formulated by Ribera to mock the Protestants! It was Ribera who taught that the "hindrance" was the Holy Spirit. Sound familiar? If it was the Holy Spirit, Paul would have boldly said so, since he had no hesitations in other chapters when writing about this subject.[52] I will conclude this section with a few more historic quotes.

> *Tertullian: We pray for the Roman Emperors and empire, for we know that convulsions and calamities are threatening the whole world, and the end of the world itself, is kept back by the intervention of the Roman empire.*
>
> *Jerome: The Roman world rushes to destruction, and we bend not our neck in humiliation…The hindrance in antichrist's way is removing, and we heed it not…In that one city the whole world hath fallen.*
>
> *Evangrius: The Roman emperors are driven from their kingdoms: wars rage: all is commotion: Antichrist must be at hand.*

In conclusion, we see that Paul had good reason for refusing to openly name the hindrance; to do so would have brought swift and terrible destruction to the infant Church in Thessalonica. He had already caused a disturbance when he was there speaking against Caesar. "Remember you not, that, when I was with you, I told you these things?"[53]

---

52 Hindrance information taken from Thomas Foster's The Antichrist—Who Is He?

53 II Thessalonians 2:5

The Temple of the Man of Sin

The teaching of a literal rebuilt Temple in Jerusalem is a pillar in the futurist school of Bible prophecy (Ribera's school). Ribera was forced to teach this doctrine because the reformers understood that Paul's "Man of Sin" would sit in a spiritual Temple. The futurists need a literal Temple to house their single Antichrist which they teach will appear exclusively at the end of the age. This pillar of futurism is very easily destroyed with truth. Therefore, let's lay the axe to the root of this rotten and erroneous tree.

Second Thessalonians 2:3-4

v.3 Let no man deceive you by any means: for that day shall not come, except there come a falling away first, and that man of sin be revealed, the son of perdition:

v.4 Who opposeth and exalteth himself above all that is called God, or that is worshipped; so that he as God sitteth in the temple of God, shewing himself that he is God.

In the Greek language, there are two different words translated "temple." They are **naos** and **hieron**. The apostle Paul was very careful not to confuse the meanings in his epistles. After Pentecost, in the Book of Acts and in the rest of the New Testament, any time the literal Temple (building) is referred to, the word hieron is used. For example, "Now Peter and John went up together into the hieron at the hour of prayer..." However, in First Corinthians 6:19 Paul states, "What, know ye not that your body is the naos of the Holy Ghost?" And in Ephesians 2:19-20; "Ye are of the household of God and are built on the foundation of the apostles and prophets, Jesus Christ being the chief corner-stone; in whom all the building, fitly framed together, groweth unto an holy naos in the Lord." The distinction is absolutely clear. After Acts chapter two, the word hieron is used to identify the literal building and is referenced over twenty times. However, naos is exclusively used to identify the person in-dwelt by the Holy Ghost. Clearly, our bodies are the New Testatment Temple.

Futurist writer Dr. A.J. Gordon wrote: "There is no undisputed instance in the New Testament where this word naos is applied to the Jewish temple."[54]

Many early patristic expositors understood the applicability of the

54 George H. Clement, The ABC of the Prophetical Scriptures, p. 63.

figure to the New Testament Christian body. Hilary and Jerom, Chrysostom and Theodoret, explained it of the Christian professing Church; and Ambrose and Augustine... Many Romish expositors too of a later date held the same view as Jerom and Theodoret."[55]

Now for the necessary adjustment in our thinking. Which word is used by Paul when warning the Thessalonian Church? NAOS (II Thess. 2:4). This is the only Temple that antichrist desires. Paul emphatically tells us that the Man of Sin will sit in the spiritual Temple. With his blasphemies, he will debase it!

Remember, Paul said the man of sin would:

> *...exalt himself above all that is called a god, or that is worshiped; so that he sits in the Temple of the God, showing himself that he is a god (II Thess. 2:4, Literal Greek).*

This man would show himself to be equal with God, possessing the attributes of God. Did the popes ever make such claims? Yes, they did. History books are full of quotes that could be given. Here is an excerpt from the infamous Bull "Unam Sanctam":

> *The Roman Pontiff judges all men, but is judged by no one...We declare, assert, define and pronounce to be subject to the Roman Pontiff is to every creature altogether necessary for salvation... that which was spoken of Christ, "Thou has subdued all things under His feet," may well seem verified in me...I have the authority of the King of Kings. I am all in all, and above all, so that God Himself and I, the Vicar of God, have but one consistory, and I am able to do almost all that God can do. What therefore, can you make of me but God? (Pope Boniface VIII, 1303)*

In his work, The Approaching End of the Age, Guinness lists shocking excerpts from Fox's Acts and Monuments. Extracts are given from two hundred and twenty-three authentic documents, comprising decrees, decretals, extravagants, pontificals, and bulls, all of which are indisputable evidence. The Scripture states that "he that exhalteth himself shall be abased " and who can match the self-exaltation of the Roman pontiffs? The following are excerpts of papal arrogance from Fox's volume of evidence:

> *Wherefore, seeing such power is given to Peter, and to me...emperors themselves, ought to subdue their executions to me; only I am subject to no creature, no, not to myself...for no canon bindeth me... and who obeyeth not me is a heretic. I am greater than the angels...*

---

55 Horae Apocalypticae, vol III, p. 90.

and have power to bind and loose in heaven...so it is to be affirmed, that the Vicar of Christ hath power on things celestial, terrestrial, and infernal [heaven, earth and hell], which he took immediately of Christ... And likewise it is to be presumed that the bishop of that church is always holy. Yea, though he fall into homicide or adultery, he may sin, but yet he cannot be accused, but rather excused by the murders of Samson, and the thefts of the Hebrews, etc.[56]

When has Rome ever renounced these blasphemous sayings? I would like to see it in writing, signed by any papal authority! Simply stated, a church which claims infallibility cannot repent. Paul wasn't mincing his words when he said that this man would be a "Man of Sin"! This is the same man who had fooled many Protestants with further blasphemous teachings, such as the doctrine of the "Immaculate Conception." Many ministers misunderstand this wicked doctrine and assume that it relates to the virgin birth of Christ. However, it is a teaching about Mary's own birth:

We declare, pronounce and define that the Most Blessed Virgin Mary, at the first instant of her conception was preserved immaculate from all stain of original sin, by the singular grace and privilege of the Omnipotent God, in the virtue of the merits of Jesus Christ, the Savior of Mankind, and that this doctrine was revealed by God, and therefore must be believed firmly and constantly by all the faithful.[57]

Note what Daniel prophesied concerning this arrogant little horn; he said that it would have "a mouth speaking great things"! (Dan. 7:8)

I believe enough has been presented to reveal the Man of Sin. The correct interpretation of the "Temple" doctrine alone creates massive problems for futurists and dispensationalists. I believe a severe blow has been struck to Ribera's hermeneutics. This hellish domination of Jesuit thought in the realm of prophetic teaching must be removed from the minds of God's true flock. The ever present fear of Antichrist is like a cancer in the body of believers waiting to take its toll. It must be cut out by the sharp, unsheathed, two-edged sword of truth.

The Bible teaches a restoration of all things, and the uninterrupted growth of the kingdom (Dan. 2:35) before Christ's bodily return. However, the futurists teach a destruction of all things by the Antichrist before Christ returns triumphant. Daniel said, "Many shall be purified and made white, and tried; but the wicked shall do wickedly: and none

56 Guinness, pp. 189-191.

57 Papal Bull, "Ineffabilus Deus," quoted in "The Tablet," December 12, 1953.

of the wicked shall understand; but the wise shall understand."[58]

The Jesuit order is one of the most sinister institutions on the face of the earth. To deny this fact leads us into certain darkness. Why do we allow them to instruct us on prophetic interpretation? Will we have the courage to face this issue? It undoubtedly will, like many other volatile issues in the body of Christ, separate the men of God from the fearful and unbelieving. Have we forgotten the Reformation? Have we forgotten the Inquisition? What would the martyrs of these two tumultuous eras have to say to us today? God has not forgotten. "Great Babylon came in remembrance before God, to give unto her cup of the wine of the fierceness of his wrath."[59] God is raising up a wave of ministers who will guide the Church in remembering what He considers to be very relevant issues which have not been righteously judged by this present generation.

---

58 Daniel 12:10

59 Revelation 16:19

Thomas Newton's Year-Day Principle

It is important to understand the terms used in Scripture for the fulfillment of prophecy. Are the days and years always literal, or are they often symbolic? The answer is to be found in examining the context. This is essential. A text without its context is only a pretext.

In short-term prophecies the years mentioned are sometimes literal years. For example we read, "and within three score and five years shall Ephraim be broken, that it be not a people" (Isaiah 7:8). In this instance the time measure was fulfilled in literal years, since the house of Israel went into captivity to Assyria within sixty-five years as prophesied.

There is no disagreement between Roman Catholic and Protestant scholars when it comes to Daniel's seventy weeks. All agree that each day is to be interpreted as a year. The futurists are forced to accept the fact that the prophetical seventy weeks are interpreted a year for a day, but they struggle with other vital Divine time measures. For example:

IN DANIEL	
That of the domination of the little horn	Dan. 7:24
That of the desolation of the sanctuary	Dan. 8:14
Time, times, and a half	Dan. 12:5,9
The period of 1290 days	Dan. 12:11
The period of 1335 days	Dan. 12:12
IN THE APOCALYPSE	
The ten days' tribulation of the church at Smyrna	Rev. 2:10
The duration of the scorpion torment	Rev. 9:5
The career of the Euphratean horsemen	Rev. 9:15
The time of the down-treading of the Holy City	Rev. 11:2
That of the prophesying of the two witnesses	Rev. 11:3
The time they lay unburied	Rev. 11:9
The sojourn of the woman in the wilderness	Rev. 12:6,14
The period of the domination of the beast	Rev. 13:6

The futurists attempt to interpret these days as literal days. Of course, if we believe that the entire Book of Revelation is restricted to Ribera's seven-year tribulation period, then we have no alternative but to defend the inconsistent day-day theory. However, Protestant theology has understood for centuries the day-for-a-year principle. A brilliant example of this is seen in the writings of Bishop Thomas Newton.

In Bishop Newton's exhaustive work, The Dissertations on the Prophecies,[60] he looked at the 2300 days of Daniel 8:13-14.

v.13 Then I heard one saint speaking, and another saint said unto that certain saint which spake, How long shall be the vision concerning the daily sacrifice, and the transgression of desolation, to give both the sanctuary and the host to be trodden under foot?

v.14 And he said unto me, Unto two thousand and three hundred days; then shall the sanctuary be cleansed.

Bishop Newton understood the Grecian implication necessary to commence the time measure (he wrote in 1754). He calculated 2300 years from his interpreted starting date of 334 B.C., (Alexander the Great's invading Asia, Anno Mundi 3670) and said that 2300 years later we should see the Jews restored to Palestine and the Temple site regained by them. Worked out, this would have to transpire by 1967. The futurist laughed and said it would never happen, but it did! The prophecy was fulfilled with the Six Days' War of 1967 when the Jews again took control of the Temple site after exactly 2300 years of its being "trodden under foot"! What an amazing prediction, precisely fulfilled. Doesn't this put to shame the futurist date setters of our time? I quote from Kessing's Contemporary Archives:

In one of the most rapid and dramatic campaigns in modern history, Israel achieved within eighty hours a complete military victory over her Arab opponents before all hostilities ceased on 10 June...Israel had by the end of the Six Days' War (1) overrun the entire Sinai Peninsula... (2) gained control of the old city of Jerusalem, with the result that the whole of Jerusalem came under Jewish control for the first time in nearly 2,000 years [actually, as we have already established, it was 2,300 years]...

What a victory for the Jews, and right on time. At the end of the 2300 years of Daniel 8:14, the sanctuary site was won back. God has His Divine time for everything, and He is never late. As Daniel 5:21 tells us, the Most High God rules in the kingdom of men. Why have we forsaken the "more sure word of prophecy"?

---

60 Thomas Newton, The Dissertations on the Prophecies, pp. 290-91.

334 B.C. .... 1967 A.D.

2300 DAY-YEARS

PERFECT!

Biblical commentator Adam Clarke likewise addressed the 2300 days and came to the same conclusions. However, he made a mathematical error in his calculations and concluded the time measure in 1966, instead of the proper fulfillment date of 1967. We must remember that when one is calculating from B.C. to A.D., one year is lost in the overlap. This was Clarke's mistake. Nevertheless, this man understood the year-day principle and openly proclaimed it as true prophetic interpretation. We read from his commentary:

> *I think the prophetic day should be understood here, as in other parts of this prophet, and must signify so many years. If we date these years from the vision of the he goat (Alexander's invading Asia), this was A.M. 3670, B.C. 334; and two thousand three hundred years from that time will reach to A.D. 1966, or one hundred and forty-one years from the present A.D. 1825.*[61]

Remarkably, these men pointed to our generation and proclaimed prophetic fulfillment. To them, prophecy was a "sure word." Today's futurist teachers are far from sure! Their books are full of erroneous dates and scenarios. When their teachings are put to scholastic interrogation, they crumble into incoherent puzzle pieces.

I think it is appropriate to add to our list of questions. It is impossible to travel along this path of historical disclosure and reject the blatantly obvious questions that are arising in our minds. I can't list them all, but I can present some very serious problems for futuristic theologians.

1. If the year-day theory is applicable to part of the Book of Daniel, i.e., the seventy weeks, then what about the rest of the time measures in his prophecies? By what authority do you pick and choose?
2. The Apostle John incorporates Daniel's time measures into the Revelation. Are they not subject to the same consistent interpretation?
3. Therefore, are the Revelation's seals, trumpets and vials yet to be fulfilled in Ribera's "seven year tribulation period," or have they transpired throughout the Church Age? If so, where are we today? When were they fulfilled?

---

61 Adam Clarke, Clarke Commentary, vol. IV. p. 598.

Remember, to teach futuristic or preterist eschatological interpretations is to teach schools of thought birthed by the Roman Catholic church. Lord, let this present darkness be removed from our eyes, that we may see how you have asserted the credibility of Your Word upon the written prophets and their prophecies (one third of the Bible).

Thus far we have challenged the very foundations of a prophetic "Empire of Superstition." All of the previous history and accompanying accusations were necessary so that we might understand what is at (the) stake, waiting to be burned up. I boast in nothing. Good men of God have spent their ministries trying to interpret these mysteries, unfortunately never obtaining the necessary keys of knowledge. They have established themselves as teachers, and now must face the possibility of becoming children in this debate within the body. It will not be easy, and I do not rejoice in the fear and heartache that inevitably accompanies theological reformations. Nevertheless, we must press on. The prophet Jeremiah understood this type of ministry. His commission was clear: ***"to root out, and to pull down, and to destroy, and to throw down, to build and to plant."***[62]

Already I have obeyed, in moderation, the first of these commands. Now it is time to "build and plant." Before we interpret the seventy weeks, let's heed the words of H. Grattan Guinness:

> *One of the gravest evils of futurism is the terrible way in which it tampers with this great fundamental prophecy (Daniel 9:27), applying to the future doings of some ideal Antichrist, its Divine description of the past deeds of the historic Christ.*
>
> *He (Antichrist) co-exists not with a recognized Jewish nation, but with the rejection and dispersion of the Jews, and with a recognized professing Christian Church. His sphere is not Palestine, but Christendom; his throne is not Jerusalem but Rome; his victims are not Jews, but Christians...* [63]

---

62 Jeremiah 1:10

63 H. Grattan Guinness, Approaching End of the Age.

Interlude: Futurist Teaching

Futurist Teaching

It is now necessary that we briefly examine some major themes of futurism. This is imperative, because an entire systematic theology is going to crumble before our eyes as we see the true interpretation of Daniel's vision. Admittedly, I will not do justice to their theories, or to all the "in-house" variations thereof. I simply desire to equip you with a basic understanding. Should you desire to research futurism, you'll have no problem finding the futurist scheme in Christian bookstores. Unfortunately, it reigns preeminent.

Throughout the first sixty-nine prophetical weeks, many of the futurists and historicists agree, accurately dating the beginning of the weeks in the year 457 B.C. and ending the sixty-ninth week (483 years later) in 27 A.D. with the baptism of Jesus in the river Jordan (the appearing of Messiah the Prince).

The following informative excerpt concerning the dating of Christ's birth is from the Thompson Chain-Reference Bible, 5th Improved Edition. p. 1655:

> *The Romans, who were the dominating power when Jesus was born, generally dated all events from the foundation of Rome, Anno Urbis I.*
>
> *In the sixth century the Pope determined to have a new calendar prepared which would date all events from the birth of Jesus. [Remember, Daniel said that the little horn would, "think to change times and laws" (Dan. 7:25).]*
>
> *He commissioned a monk, named Dionysius, to do the work.*
>
> *This calendar, when finished, was gradually adopted throughout Christendom.*
>
> *Modern scholars have found that some of the dates of Roman History near the beginning of the Christian Era cannot be reconciled with the calendar of Dionysius. For example, according to the Roman annals, Herod the Great, who ruled Judea when Jesus was born, died in the year 750 Anno Urbis. Dionysius placed the birth of Jesus in the year 754 Anno Urbis, in apparent contradiction of well established dates of Roman records.*
>
> *Jesus was probably born in 749 or 750 Anno Urbis, that is, four or five years earlier than the date given in our commonly accepted calendar.*

Hence, in modern literature, scholars refer to Christmas as 4 or 5 B.C. [Most lean heavily to 4 B.C.; I agree with this conclusion.]

Some of the futurists like to date the decree which commenced the time measure a little later than 457 B.C., trying to bring the conclusion of the 483 years to the crucifixion (30 A.D.). They know that the crucifixion is involved in the prophecy. This presents a great problem for them, but they don't mention that! They simply take liberty with established and tried historical dates so as to make their (Ribera's) schemes fit.

After the sixty-ninth week, they say that the clock stops and the final week is separated into the future. They have now broken a time measure. They often refer to this as their "Parentheses Theory." The Antichrist does not appear until this time, their "Great Tribulation."

Not only do they put the Antichrist exclusively in the future, but they try to tell us that the seals, trumpets and vials of the Book of Revelation transpire during this period! Why would Jesus reveal Himself only to the last prophetic week of this age? And then they try to tell us that it is those who are left on the earth after the rapture who will interpret these terrible judgments! This doesn't agree with what Daniel taught. He said that "none of the wicked shall understand."

Finally, futurists teach that "tribulation" and "wrath" are added to the 70th week. Some teach the first three and a half years as tribulation, and the second half of this terrible period, wrath. The "rapture" of the Church has various interpretations within the framework of this most eventful week:

Pre-tribulationists—put the rapture at the beginning of the week.

Post-tribulationists—put the rapture at the end of the week.

And some put it in the middle of the week (mid-weekers). Regardless of their rapture theories, they all revolve around the seventieth week of Daniel's time measure occurring in the future at the end of the Age. The teachers of this Roman theology are numerous.

And to make things worse, some futurists teach three very perplexing scenarios pertaining to the rule of their Antichrist:

1. *He will be a political leader arising out of the Common Market or Syria. This has already been refuted by the apostle John in First John 2:18-19.*
2. *He signs a peace treaty with Israel.*
3. *When the Russians invade natural Israel, according to futurists' interpretations of Ezekiel chapters 38 and 39, Joel chapters 2*

> *and 3 and Zechariah chapters 12 and 13, Antichrist is the one who defeats them!*

However, I find this scenario to be very troublesome. If one reads these aforementioned chapters, he cannot help but come to the conclusion that God, using what instruments He desires, defeats these armies.

I believe this is a sufficient summary of Ribera's teachings. Let's search the Word of God and prove the beginning and fulfillment of this great prophecy. Why are the seventy weeks so important? I believe that there are three critical reasons:

First, the seventy weeks is one of the greatest Messianic prophecies recorded in the Bible. With its understanding, the exact year that Messiah the Prince began His public ministry, confirming the New Covenant with the Jews for seven years, would be known. This proves that Jesus was Israel's predicted Messiah.

Secondly, the futuristic school of Bible prophecy totally depends on Ribera's interpretation of Daniel chapter nine. If the truth of the time measure is taught, this whole school of deception will come crumbling down at our feet. No longer will Kingdom and Restorational teachings be hindered by the escapist and defeatist mentality of the dispensationalists. A great breach will be repaired!

Thirdly, once futurism is sent back to the pit from where it originated, we can properly interpret the Apocalypse. I do not believe that the New Testament revolves exclusively around a two-generation Church. There have been two millenniums of life and death struggle in Christendom between these periods. Don't tell me that our Lord had nothing to say to these saints! Many know better, and can prove His prophetic word to them.

Part Four
The True Interpretation

Six Messianic Prophecies

The study of Bible prophecy will always be a strong attraction for the believer. There is a powerful element of curiosity present in our human nature. Jesus addressed this gift when He commanded us to "search the scriptures." Unfortunately, some ministers will shun prophetic study and seek to defend their indifferent positions in a variety of ways. Some excuses are very clever. Nevertheless, we are commanded to declare "all the counsel of God." I acknowledge that eschatology has been made increasingly difficult by the flood of various interpretations. That is why it is essential that we grasp the keys of knowledge pertaining to the prophetic and build carefully and accurately with them. I hope this unfolding interpretation of the seventy weeks will arm even the elementary prophetic minister or student with the most important key available, the truth!

Keep in mind that the futuristic interpretation was never considered for over fifteen centuries. It did not penetrate into Protestant theology for another three. A cloud of witnesses refused to entertain such twisting of the Scriptures, especially since the source was no secret!

The change in interpretation would have been all right if it were a revelation from God for the end of the age, but it wasn't; it was a deceptive teaching from Ribera.

TO FINISH THE TRANSGRESSION

Isaiah 53:5 states, "He was wounded for our transgressions." In Daniel 9:11 we read that "all Israel have transgressed thy law" but the unmatched height of this transgression occurred at Calvary, when Israel crucified her Messiah. Adam Clarke comments that this was "to finish (lechalle, to restrain) the transgression, which was effected by the preaching of the Gospel, and pouring of the Holy Ghost upon men."

TO MAKE AN END OF SINS

Matthew 1:21 states, "He shall save his people from their sins." In Hebrews 9:26 we read, "But now once in the end of the world hath He appeared to put away sin by the sacrifice of himself." Adam Clarke expounded beautifully on these very vital aspects of the prophecy and I again quote him. "To make an end of sins; rather ulehathem chataoth, 'to make an end of sin offering' which our Lord did when he offered his spotless soul and body on the cross once and for all."

On Calvary, Christ was numbered with the transgressors; but He was there for the vast transgressions of His people. It was there that He was wounded for our transgressions and bruised for our iniquities. Who can doubt that His perfect atonement made an end of the need for future sin offerings?

TO MAKE RECONCILIATION FOR INIQUITY

In Second Corinthians 5:19 the apostle Paul proclaims, "God was in Christ, reconciling the world unto himself..." Paul states again in Romans 5:10, "For if when we were enemies, we were reconciled to God by the death of his Son..." Clarke teaches that He made "reconciliation (ulechapper, 'to make atonement for expiation') for iniquity: which he did by the once offering up of himself."

It is almost unbelievable to think that some would put these events into the future, yet to be fulfilled by the Antichrist. Impossible, you say. No. Unfortunately, it's reality. Some futurist writers have tried to tell us this. By placing this great event in the future they nullify the proclamation of Christ's reconciliation! Christ came not only to atone, but likewise to reconcile. This He fulfilled. Don't let anybody tell you otherwise.

TO BRING IN EVERLASTING RIGHTEOUSNESS

Second Corinthians 5:21 states, "For he hath made him to be sin for us, who knew no sin; that we might be made the righteousness of God in him." The great "Prince of Preachers," Spurgeon, declared, "One of the main designs of Christ's coming to earth was to bring in everlasting righteousness." The futurist school casts all these blessings into a future millennium, but Jesus has become to the Christian his righteousness (I Cor. 1:30). Paul made it clear that the Kingdom of God was "righteousness and peace, and joy in the Holy Ghost" (Rom. 14:17). In the Old Testament, the prophet Isaiah foretold of this righteousness which would be "forever" (Isa. 51:8). And Jeremiah speaks of the "Lord our righteousness" (Jer. 23:5-6).

TO SEAL UP THE VISION AND PROPHECY

Isaiah 29:10-11

v.10 For the Lord hath poured out upon you the spirit of deep sleep, and hath closed your eyes: the prophets and your rulers, and the seers hath he covered.

v.11 And the vision of all is become unto you as the words of a book that is sealed, which men deliver to one that is learned, saying, Read this, I pray thee: and he saith, I cannot; for it is sealed.

When Isaiah used the word "sealed" here, he used it in the same context as did the prophet Daniel when writing about the king's seal on the lion's den (Dan. 6:17). It meant "to close up tightly"!

Because of Israel's refusal to listen and to heed the words of the prophets, finally rejecting the Lord Himself, their judgment would be a terrible blindness that would tightly seal up the Scriptures to their understanding. Paul elaborates on this theme in Second Corinthians 3:14-15:

> *v.14 But their minds were blinded: for until this day remaineth the same veil untaken away in the reading of the old testament; which veil is done away in Christ.*
>
> *v.15 But even unto this day, when Moses is read, the veil is upon their heart.*

Again, because of Israel's cry, "His blood be on us, and on our children," part of their judgment was a blindness to what the prophets wrote concerning their Messiah.

TO ANOINT THE MOST HOLY

The scriptural evidence which points to Christ on this issue is unshakable. Christ alone fulfilled this prophecy. Look at what the Scriptures say: "Therefore also that holy thing which shall be born of thee shall be called the Son of God" (Luke 1:35). Luke again records, "The Spirit of the Lord is upon me, because he hath anointed me to preach the gospel to the poor..." (4:18) In Acts 10:38 it is proclaimed, "God anointed Jesus of Nazareth with the Holy Ghost and with power." Finally, we gain from Adam Clarke's insight, "And to anoint the most holy, kodesh kodashim, 'the Holy of holies', mashac, to anoint, (from which come mashiach, the Messiah, the anointed one)."[64]

I stand defiant of any teacher or expositor who applies these holy prophecies to any other than Jesus Himself! Why were the seventy weeks determined? To finish the transgression; to make an end of sins; to make reconciliation for iniquity; to bring in everlasting righteousness; to seal up the vision and prophecy; and to anoint the Most Holy!

---

64 Adam Clarke's Commentary provides a wonderful insight to these six vital prophetic points. I recommend the reader examine his arguments for further understanding. These points of prophecy are very important and beautiful admonitions concerning "Messiah the Prince," not some antichrist prince!

The Time Measure

We must now ascertain what commandments were involved regarding the Jews' return from their exile in Babylon. Both Nehemiah and Ezra describe the history of those restoration events. It is vitally important that we interpret them correctly. Daniel was given the admonition that a "specific" event would begin the historical unfolding of the seventy weeks. If this event is not exactly sixty-nine weeks (483 years) before Christ's ministerial advent "unto Messiah the Prince," the prophecy is void.

Daniel 9:25

Know therefore and understand, that from the going forth of the commandment to restore and to build Jerusalem unto the Messiah the Prince shall be seven weeks [49 years +], and threescore and two weeks [434 years]...

In the year 538 B.C., Cyrus made a decree which is recorded in Ezra 1:2-3:

v.2 Thus sayeth Cyrus king of Persia, The Lord god of heaven hath given me all the kingdoms of the earth; and he hath charged me to build him a house at Jerusalem, which is in Judah.

v.3 Who is there among you of all his people? His God be with him, and let him go up to Jerusalem, which is in Judah, and build the house of the Lord God of Israel...

Many have tried to teach us that this was the prophetic commandment which began this great time measure; however, this is impossible!

The prophecy tells us that from the time a certain commandment would go forth to rebuild Jerusalem — not the Temple — to the advent of Messiah would be 7 + 62 weeks. This equals a period of 69 prophetic weeks, or 483 days. Using the day-for-a-year principle taught in Ezekiel 4:6, "I have appointed thee each day for a year," we have 483 prophetical days, equivalent to 483 years.

With the decree of Cyrus, the captives' objective was to rebuild the Temple. However, the command which would begin the seventy weeks would be one to restore and build Jerusalem, not the Temple!

If we proceed 483 years from Cyrus' decree in 538 B.C., it will take us to the year 55 B.C. Messiah the Prince did not appear at this time. Jesus appeared at the river Jordan in the year 27 A.D. Therefore, if we are determined to use Cyrus' decree as the starting point, then we are forced to acknowledge an 81-year mistake in calculation! The accuracy and glory of God and His prophecy are then destroyed. This is what Ribera did. However, if we can find the proper command that signaled the beginning of the time measure, we are on our way to interpreting this prophecy with the exactness that our God intended. He doesn't need us to twist dates and times to help Him fulfill His prophetic word.

Cyrus' Decree	***No Messiah***	***Messiah Here!***
538 B.C......(483 years)....... 55 B.C.	.... 81-year gap	.........27 A.D.

PROBLEM!

Ezra 7:11-13:

Now this is the...letter that King Artaxerxes gave unto Ezra...I make a decree, that all they of the people of Israel... which are minded of their own freewill to go up to Jerusalem, go with thee.

The majority of historians and Bible scholars date this decree at 457 B.C. If we apply 483 years from the time of this decree we arrive at the year 27 A.D., the very year, according to the Christian calendar, that Jesus began His ministry. As you can see, God doesn't make 81-year mistakes. If dates don't match exactly it isn't the Word that is wrong, but rather the interpreter. We must remember that on our present calendar (previously discussed), Jesus was born in the year 4 B.C., thus making Him 30 years of age in 27 A.D. In Luke 3:22-23 we read, "The Holy Ghost descended upon him. Jesus was about thirty years of age."

So in the year 27 A.D., which was "69 weeks" or "483 years" from Artaxerxes' commandment, we have this prophetic announcement:

Jesus came into Galilee, preaching the gospel of the kingdom of God, and saying, The time is fulfilled ... (Mark 1:14-15)

What time was Jesus talking about? This fulness of time was mandated by the seventy weeks. Messiah could not appear until 483 years had elapsed from Artaxerxes' decree. This prophecy Christ fulfilled. The seventieth week had arrived! Jesus appeared at the Jordan right on time! Our God is precise in His prophetic word.

457 B.C................................483 years unto	.... 27 A.D.
Artaxerxes' decree	***Messiah the Prince***

PERFECT!

Again, our Lord displays His brilliance by further segmenting the phases of historical fulfillment within the time measure.

Daniel 9:25

...the street shall be built again and the wall, even in troublous times.

The first sixty-nine weeks of the time measure is announced as containing an initial "seven week" or "49-year" period. Why did God specify this time? Again, we turn to history and look for the exact fulfillment of this portion of the time measure.

There was a period of restoration and repairing of Jerusalem fulfilled with the administrations of Ezra and Nehemiah. They worked for 49 years in restoring the sacred constitutions and civil establishment of the Jews. This period extended from 457 B.C. to 408 B.C. Also, Daniel tells us that the streets and the walls shall be built in troubled times. Let's see if this event was incorporated during the exclusive 49-year period as prophesied.

Nehemiah 4:17

They which builded on the wall, and they that bare burdens, with those that laded, every one with one of his hands wrought in the work, and with the other hand held a weapon.

It took Nehemiah and company 52 days to build the walls. They were built in time of trouble. There was opposition by "Sanballat, and Tobiah, and the Arabians, and the Ammonites, and the Ashdodites..." (Neh. 4:7)

The building of the walls was one of Nehemiah's main missions. Several verses of Scripture verify this.

Nehemiah 2:8,13,17

v.8 And a letter unto Asaph the keeper of the king's forest, that he may give me timber to make beams for the gates of the palace which appertained to the house, and for the WALL of the city...

v.13 And I went out by night by the gate of the valley...and viewed the WALLS of Jerusalem...

v.17 Then said I unto them...come, and let us build up the WALL of Jerusalem, that we be no more a reproach.

Thus the first 49 years of the prophecy transpired even containing the manifestation of struggle that Gabriel had said would occur.

457 B.C..................49 years of troubled building.............408 B.C.

PERFECT!

Before we proceed, I want to emphasize the theme of this great prophecy. The seventy weeks revolve around Messiah the Prince, what the Jews did to Him when He appeared, and the judgment of God upon the Jews for "cutting off" Messiah the Prince. It is very important that we grasp this revelation.

It is interesting to note that Messiah is not called "King" at this point, but rather "Prince." This prophecy predicted the earthly ministry of the Messiah. If He were destined to totally displace all earthly rule at His first appearing, then the title "King" would have been appropriate. Instead, He is called a Prince. Here are five examples in the New Testament where Jesus is referred to as a Prince:

1. *Acts 3:15— "And killed the Prince of life, whom God hath raised from the dead..."*
2. *Acts 5:31— "Him hath God exalted with His right hand to be a Prince and a Saviour, for to give repentance to Israel and forgiveness of sins."*
3. *Hebrews 2:10— "For it became him, for whom are all things, and by whom are all things, in bringing many sons unto glory, to make the captain [prince] of their salvation perfect through sufferings."*
4. *Hebrews 12:2— "Looking unto Jesus, the author [prince] and finisher of our faith; who for the joy that was set before him endured the cross, despising the shame, and is set down at the right hand of the throne of God."* [65]
5. *Finally, Peter proclaimed to the Jews at Jerusalem who were responsible for "cutting off" their Messiah, "Ye denied the Holy One and the Just, and desired a murderer to be granted unto you; and killed the Prince of life..." (Acts 3:14-15)*

Daniel 9:26

And after threescore and two [62] weeks shall Messiah be cut off [the crucifixion], but not for himself: and the people of the prince that shall come shall destroy the city and the sanctuary [temple]...

In this verse we read that after the 62-week period (which naturally follows the first 7 weeks) the Messiah shall be cut off, but not for Himself (one of the most beautiful admonitions in Scripture). The words "cut off" speak of the abrupt and untimely nature of Messiah's death. The prophet Isaiah is even more graphic when he cries, "He was cut off out of the

65 Philip Mauro, The Seventy Weeks and the Great Tribulation, p. 67.

land of the living…" (Isa. 53:8) And immediately the angel states that there will be a punishment by the prince of the people that shall come.

I believe that Prince Titus, the son of Vespasian, is clearly intended, and "the people of that prince" were the Romans who, according to this prophecy, destroyed the sanctuary.

Remember that Jesus quoted Daniel nine (Matthew 24:15), and told the Jews that their house would be left unto them desolate because of their rejection of Him. This is exactly what happened under the Roman Prince Titus in 70 A.D. The siege of Jerusalem began under Titus' father Vespasian in 66 A.D. He was summoned back to Rome to become Emperor after the death of Nero's successor, Galba, leaving Titus to be in charge of the final stages of the siege. Thus, General Titus now became a Prince of Rome! The Word of God never fails in its timing and accuracy.

Prince Titus took command with his people (the Romans) and laid Jerusalem waste. However, the futurists tell us that this prince is yet to come, and this prince wasn't Titus, but rather a future Antichrist yet to come. Sir Robert Anderson even entitled his futuristic book, *The Coming Prince*. Nevertheless, I believe the interpretation is sure. This prince could be no other than Prince Titus. It has already taken place. Why do we look for another?

Daniel 9:27

And he [Messiah the Prince] shall confirm the covenant [New Covenant] with many [Daniel's people, the Jews exclusively] for one week [7 years]: and in the midst of the week he shall cause the sacrifice and the oblation to cease [Calvary], and for the overspreading of abominations he shall make it desolate, even until the consummation…

Daniel said that after 62 weeks Messiah would be cut off. Now we have the exact time of this cutting off— "in the midst of the week," or after three and a half years of ministry.

The covenant that Messiah "confirmed" or ratified could be no other than the New Covenant. There was only one covenant for which Israel waited, and it was promised in Jeremiah 31:31-33:

v.31 Behold, the days come, saith the Lord, that I will make a new covenant with the house of Israel, and with the house of Judah:

v.32 Not according to the covenant that I made with their fathers in the day that I took them by the hand to bring them out of the land of Egypt; which my covenant they brake, although I was a husband unto them, saith the Lord:

v.33 But this shall be the covenant that I will make with the house of Israel; After those days, saith the Lord, I will put my law in their inward parts, and write it in their hearts; and will be their God and they shall be my people.

Before He died, Jesus proclaimed:

And he took the cup, and gave thanks, and gave it to them, saying, Drink ye all of it; for this is My blood of the covenant, which is shed for many for the remission of sins (Matt. 26:27-28).

And Paul writes in Romans 15:8:

Now I say that Jesus Christ was a minister of the circumcision for the truth of God, to confirm the promises made unto the fathers...

The Scriptures seem to be quite clear on this very important point. The covenant referred to by the prophet Daniel was the New Covenant and it was Jesus who confirmed it, not some Antichrist in the future who makes a covenant with just the Jews in Palestine. What rubbish!

457 B.C.... 408 B.C........27 A.D..........Midst Calvary .....Final Half?
***Decree* Trouble unto {Messiah's confirming of covenant}**

GETTING INTERESTING!

I believe the following Scriptures will help set the stage for the unveiling of the true ending of the time measure. This covenant must be confirmed with the Jews exclusively for seven years. If this was not done, then there is an inaccuracy in the written prophetic Word and our Bible is futile!

Matthew 10:5

These twelve Jesus sent forth, and commanded them, saying, Go not into the way of the Gentiles, and into any city of the Samaritans enter ye not.

Also, in Romans 1:16 we read:

For I am not ashamed of the gospel of Christ: for it is the power of God unto salvation to every one that believeth; to the Jew first and also the Greek.

Why does it say "to the Jew first?" Because God said He would confirm the covenant with them for one week (the 70th week). They were given the opportunity first! This is shown time and time again throughout the Gospels.

The earthly ministry of Jesus lasted three and a half years, after which

He was crucified in the midst of the prophetic week. The veil in the Temple was rent from top to bottom, causing the Old Testament sacrifice to pass away—forever! Why do the futurists tell us that the Antichrist will cause the restored sacrifice to cease in a rebuilt Temple? They need to go back and read Hebrews chapters 8, 9 and 10.

Hebrews 8:8-10,13

v.8 Behold, the days come, saith the Lord, when I will make a new covenant with the house of Israel and with the house of Judah:

v.9 not according to the covenant that I made with their fathers in the day when I took them by the hand to lead them out of the land of Egypt; because they continued not in my covenant, and I regarded them not, saith the Lord.

v.10 For this is the covenant that I will make with the house of Israel after those days, saith the Lord...

v.13 In that he saith, A new covenant, he hath made the first old. Now that which decayeth and waxeth old is ready to vanish away.

Hebrews 9:12

Neither by the blood of goats and calves, but by his own blood he entered in once into the holy place, having obtained eternal redemption for us.

Hebrews 10:1-5,9

v.1 For the law having a shadow of good things to come, and not the very image of the things, can never with those sacrifices which they offered year by year continually make the comers thereunto perfect.

v.2 For then would they not have ceased ["he shall cause the sacrifice and the oblation to cease," (Dan. 9:27)] to be offered...

v.3 But in those sacrifices there is a remembrance again made of sins every year.

v.4 For it is not possible that the blood of bulls and goats should take away sins.

v.5 Wherefore when he cometh into the world, he saith, Sacrifice and offering ["he shall cause the sacrifice and the oblation (offering) to cease," (Dan. 9:27)] thou wouldest not...

v.9 Then said he, Lo, I come to do thy will, O God. He taketh away the first, [Who took the first away? Who caused the sacrifice and offering to cease? It is clear from the Word of God—Jesus!], that he may establish the second.

Our Lord Himself proclaimed:

"O Jerusalem, Jerusalem, thou that killest the prophets, and stonest them which are sent unto thee, how often would I have gathered thy children together, even as a hen gathereth her chickens under her wings, and ye would not! Behold, your house is left unto you desolate" (Matt. 23:37-38). Daniel 9:27 says, "and that determined shall be poured upon the desolate."

The truth of God is easily understood.

Jesus personally fulfilled the first half of the week. Now we must search the Scriptures for the revealed ending of the last half of Daniel's seventieth week. This is where an axe is laid to the root of the dispensational tree. Who desperately sought to impart this Covenant to the Jews after Christ ascended to Heaven? How long did they endeavor? How did they understand what to do, or where to go? Is this some unsolvable mystery, or is it a very understandable revelation?

The End of the Week

My friend, this whole discourse has been presented to bring us up to this climactic point. Please follow me very carefully in this matter. If we can establish the exact culmination of the prophecy, then the entire futurist school will have been successfully discredited. And if it recovers, it recovers only in the minds of men who refuse to render obeisance to the authority and revelation of the Scriptures.

After the death and resurrection of our Lord there yet remained three and a half years of this prophecy to be fulfilled. Half of the week remained to confirm this covenant with the Jews. Before He ascended into Heaven Christ commanded His disciples:

Go ye, therefore, and teach all nations... (Matt. 28:19)

This commission authorized the disciples to go out into the whole world and preach the good news of the Kingdom. However, they did not to do this immediately. They remained and preached to the Jews, and to the Jews alone. The more they preached, the more they were persecuted. This persecution came to a dramatic head with the death of the martyr Stephen.

In Acts 7:51-59, we read of Stephen's great defense of the Gospel, and his condemnation of the Jews is sharply delivered. "Christ, or nothing," was his message. They were cut to their heart, and they killed him.

*(Important Note: Stephen, the 1st martyr, was killed for giving a **history lesson.**)*

The death of Stephen is dated by most scholars three years after the crucifixion, in 33 A.D. Some have tried to end the time measure there. I don't believe this is correct. The prophecy stated that the Covenant would be confirmed for seven years exclusively to the Jews. I believe we must account for the period of transition into the next year. With the time measure beginning in 457 B.C., it cannot end until 34 A.D. Therefore we need to find the event that transpired in this year which signaled the end of the prophecy.

In Matthew 10:5 Jesus instructs His disciples:

Go not into the way of the Gentiles, and into any city of the Samaritans enter ye not.

Christ also told His disciples to "go into all the world." This is not a contradiction. The apostles understood that they were restricted by Daniel's prophecy for three and a half years after Jesus' death. At the end of that period they would be free to preach salvation to the Gentiles. How do we know this? After His resurrection, Jesus met with two men walking on the road to Emmaus. They didn't recognize Him at first. He rebuked them for not believing all that the prophets had spoken concerning Him. But in chapter 24, verse 27, Luke makes this remarkable statement:

And beginning at Moses and all the prophets, he expounded unto them in all the scriptures the things concerning himself.

We are told that the apostles were instructed in all prophecies pertaining to Christ. Revelation knowledge caused the hearts of these disciples to burn within them (v. 32). That's why they remained and preached exclusively to the Jews after receiving the "great commission." Revelation of Bible prophecy is a wonderful thing.

What did Peter and John see that signaled the end of their prophetic restriction and likewise culminated the seventy weeks? When does God make His first recorded move to the Gentiles? If the Bible reveals these scenarios, futurism can no longer claim to be the true systematic theology pertaining to eschatology (the study of last things).

The Gospel Preached in Samaria Acts 8:5

Then Philip went down to the city [region] of Samaria, and preached Christ unto them.

Why did Philip do this? Didn't he know that Christ had forbidden them to preach in Samaria (Matthew 10:15)? Did he rebel against the Lord's commandment? Did Peter and John also rebel? When they heard that the Gospel was preached in Samaria they departed as a team to establish what Philip had started. The answer is simple. They did not rebel; they were released by the Holy Spirit. It was 34 A.D., and the seventy weeks had been fulfilled The Gentiles were, for the first time, receiving the opportunity (the Kingdom message). Yes, it is just that simple!

457 B.C...34 A.D.

490 DAY-YEARS

Seven years later, Peter took the Gospel to Caesarea, to Cornelius and his entire household (Acts 10). The message of the New Covenant was proclaimed.

Then in Acts 13:46, the apostle Paul makes a very emphatic statement to the Jews in Antioch.

v.45 But when the Jews saw the multitudes, they were filled with envy, and spake against those things which were spoken by Paul, contradicting and blaspheming.

v.46 Then Paul and Barnabas waxed bold, and said, it was necessary that the word of God should first have been spoken to you: but seeing ye put it from you, and judge yourselves unworthy of everlasting life, lo, we turn to the Gentiles.

v.47 For so hath the Lord commanded us...

Why is it worded this way? Why was it "necessary" that the New Covenant message be spoken first to the Jews? Because with the Jews He confirmed His covenant for one week.

To correctly interpret the Seventy Weeks time-line prophecy, every student of Scripture must understand its impact upon the events of first century Christianity. First, it determined the timing of the coming of the Messiah. Secondly, it determined the exact timing when the Jews would receive their last call to accept the Messiah, and in their rejection, the Gospel would then be presented to ten-tribed Israel, known as "Gentiles." When Paul gave his ultimatum to the Jews at Antioch, he fulfilled the prophecy spoken to Israel by Isaiah (49:5-6) 700 years before.

As the angel Gabriel stated, "Seventy weeks are determined upon thy people and upon thy holy city." So the prophecy commenced and ended, encompassing all the necessary predictions. There is no future seven-year tribulation period to come. Therefore, truth requires that we adjust an abundance of our thinking concerning what Christ will restore in the end times; what "must" be restored according to the Word of God, and what is the role of His Kingdom now presently on this earth. God is no respecter of persons. If what we are teaching is contrary to truth, we must repent—no matter what the cost.

Acts 3:20-21

v.20 Then he will send you the Christ he has predestined, that is Jesus.

v.21 Whom heaven must keep till the universal restoration comes which God proclaimed... (Jerusalem Bible)

Will the Church be here and participate in the "universal restoration"? Since we no longer have a seven-year period in which to confine the strategy of God, what about the Bride of Christ? What is her destiny? What about the rapture?

Seventy Weeks of the Prophet Daniel — *Daniel 9:20-27*

Prophetic Scale: 1 day equals 1year: ***"I have appointed thee each day for a year"*** ***(Ezekiel 4:6)***
Each prophetic week equals 7 years

This was God's timeline for dealing with the **Judah** nation (***not*** **Israel** of the Dispersion). These 70 weeks was the ***second*** time period of 490 years in which God dealt with the **Judah** nation. The **first** time resulted in a 70-year captivity, but the **second** resulted in utter desolation. ***(2 Chronicles 36:14-21, St. Matthew 23:37-38)***

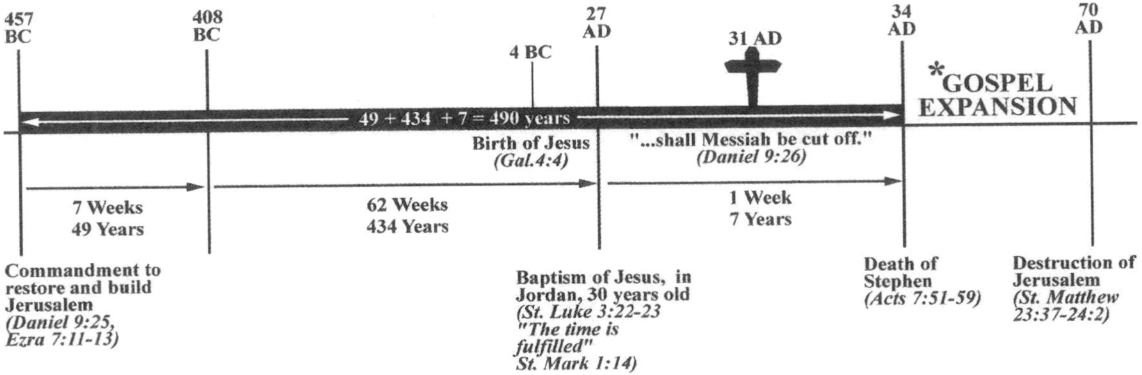

***GOSPEL EXPANSION**
Acts 8:5 **Philip was now free to preach in Samaria**
Acts 13:46 **Paul goes to the "Gentiles"**

The Messianic Purpose: *Daniel 9:24*

1. **To finish the transgression** ***(Isaiah 53:5; Hebrews 10:12-14)***
2. **To make an end of sins** ***(Hebrews 9:26)***
3. **To make reconciliation for iniquity** ***(Romans 5:10; Hebrews 10:17)***
4. **To bring in everlasting righteousness** ***(2 Corinthians 5:21)***
5. **To seal up the vision and prophecy** ***(St. Matthew 5:17)***
6. **To anoint the Most Holy** ***(St. Luke 4:18; Acts 10:38)***

Part Five
Pre-Tribulation Rapture?

Simply, Who Has the Feet?

I believe that it will be most helpful to the reader if we preface our look at the "rapture" teaching with a good, biblical perspective. A perspective is defined as "a view of things in which they are in the right relation." Since the rapture doctrine relates to the body of Christ, it will benefit us immensely if we look at what the Bible teaches about Christ's body in relation to its Head.

When writing the Ephesian church, the apostle Paul uses the example of marriage to teach a symbolic principle of the Church. He states, "For the husband is the head of the wife, even as Christ is the head of the church: and he is the saviour of the body" (Eph. 5:23). He also states that Christ is "Far above all principality, and power, and might, and dominion…And hath put all things under his feet, and gave him to be the head over all things to the church, which is his body…" (Eph. 1:21-23). In Colossians 1: la Paul writes, "And he is the head of the body, the church…" These verses of Scripture clearly reveal that Christ is the Head of His Body, the Church.

If Christ is our Head, and we are His body, it appears logical to assume that we have feet. Have you ever seen feet connected directly to a head? Of course not. Feet are attached to a body. This sounds pretty silly, I grant you; nevertheless, this simple truth has profound implications when the "rapture" of the Church is studied.

Paul ends his letter to the Roman church with this very powerful and encouraging admonition. "And the God of peace shall bruise Satan under your feet shortly" (Rom. 16:20). Again it is clear that we are the body and the possessors of feet. The day will come when all enemies are put under our feet! And what will happen when that occurs? Christ will return.

David proclaimed, "The Lord said unto my Lord, Sit thou at my right hand, until I make thine enemies thy footstool [put them under your feet]" (Ps. 110:1). In Hebrews 10:12-13 we read, "But this man, after he had offered one sacrifice for sins for ever sat down on the right hand of God; from henceforth expecting [waiting] till his enemies be made his footstool." What is Christ waiting for? He's waiting for His Bride to mature so that all enemies can be put under her feet, the feet of His body. According to the Word of God, until this is accomplished, Christ will wait, or remain in the heavens. Acts 3:20-21 is very clear on this point. It states, "And he shall send Jesus Christ, which before was preached unto you: Whom the heaven must receive until the times of restitution [restoration] of all things…"

So when does the Bible say that the end will come? Paul revealed this mystery to us in First Corinthians 15:24-25:

Then cometh the end, when he shall have delivered up the kingdom to God, even the Father; when he shall have put down all rule and all authority and power. For he must reign, till he hath put all enemies under his feet.

In this very simple discourse, the concept of a pre-tribulation rapture of the Church has been dealt a very severe jolt. As we proceed and define rapture theology, its historical origin, and its consistent opposition to our Lord's teachings, this doctrine will hopefully be put in its legitimate context. How can Christ return for His Church and still have enemies wreaking havoc on the earth? Remember also that the seven-year tribulation theory (Ribera's theory) has been completely annihilated.

When we examine the rapture teaching, John N. Darby will again appear in a preeminent position of responsibility. Darby had many serious flaws and limitations. It would be foolish to ignore these, just as it is foolish to ignore major teaching flaws of any minister. Their words must be put to the fire, not necessarily their lives. I am not attacking men of God, only what men of God have erroneously proclaimed as God's truth.

Alexander Reese very eloquently described the type of judgmental attitude which must be active in the Church. We are commanded to execute "righteous judgment."

As the Mayflower Pilgrims were about to sail for the New World in 1620, John Robinson in his address to them lamented that the Reformed Churches could go no further than the instruments of their Reformation, Luther and Calvin. He urged them "to receive whatever light or truth" should be made known from God's written Word. It was not possible, he added, "that the Christian world should come so lately out of such thick Antichristian darkness, and that full perfection of knowledge should break forth at once."[66]

The prophetic darkness of today must be eradicated through a process of restoration. "An Ever Reforming Church" was the cry of our Reformation fathers. Even so, Lord Jesus, reform and restore quickly!

Reese went further and used Darby as an example and a warning:

Then it must be said that Darby experienced the danger that comes to every teacher of the Bible: the temptation to be original; to discover

66 G.P. Fisher, History of the Christian Church, pp. 463-64.

> *and give out things not previously seen; to be wise above that which is written; to speculate and be fanciful. We all do it... The imperfection of the human mind, and its tendency to err or be fanciful, are sufficient explanation.*[67]

I have tried to abide by this above stated premise. I am not teaching or revealing anything new. Ribera taught us new things; Darby taught us new things. Christ revealed to us true things hidden from the foundation of the world. It is my contention that the rapturist doctrine opposes our Lord's teachings about the harvest at the end of the age. This flaw alone disqualifies its validity.

67 Alexander Reese, The Approaching Advent of Christ, pp. 316- 17.

Definition and Origin

Proverbs 2:21-22

For the upright shall dwell in the land, and the perfect shall remain in it. But the wicked shall be cut off from the earth, and the transgressors shall be rooted out of it.

John 17:15

I pray not that thou shouldest take them out of the world...

Many Christians today believe in the doctrine of a pre-tribulation rapture. According to this doctrine, the Second Coming of Christ will be divided into two distinct phases which are separated by a period of seven, or at least three and a half, years. During the seven-year period, this doctrine claims that the epic events of chapters six through eighteen of the Revelation will transpire. In general terms, most proponents of the doctrine refer to the seven-year dividing time as "the great tribulation" or "Daniel's 70th week." The first phase is called the "rapture" and the second, or end phase, is called the "revelation."[68]

Interpretations of the pre-tribulation rapture follow several divergent tangents. Some makers of doctrine predict three raptures, while others champion a mid-week rapture. Hal Lindsey defined the rapture as follows: "The word 'rapture' means to snatch away or take out... It will be the living end. The ultimate trip."[69] But Jesus said, "I pray not that thou shouldest take them out of the world." Who's right?

SEVEN YEARS?

Rapture?............................... Rapture? .... Rapture?
Beginning ....Middle.. End

When the doctrine of pre-tribulation rapture is exposed to the light of biblical truth, it crumbles in a shadowy heap of implied meanings and erroneous conclusions. Indeed, the word "rapture" cannot be found in the Bible, because it is not written there. Berean scrutiny[70] of God's

---

68 Proponents of this theory are already in trouble. Now that we understand that Daniel's 70th week was perfectly fulfilled, we can immediately detect the foundational flaw in the "two-phase" teaching!

69 Hal Lindsey, The Late Great Planet Earth, p. 137.

70 Acts 17:10-11

Word shows us that the doctrine of the pretribulationists was not built on a solid scriptural foundation, but instead on the shifting sands of intellect.

Neither Jesus, Paul, Peter, John, nor any writer of the Bible, taught such a theory. Notions of a pre-tribulation rapture were unknown to the early pre-Nicaean Church Fathers (e.g. Justin Martyr, 100-165; Irenaeus 130-202; Tertullian, 160-240), who were convinced that the Church would be present on the Earth during a perilous time at the end of the age.

No Protestant church creed or Reformer ever taught it. The great pillars of the Reformed faith—Wycliffe, Huss and Luther—opened the hearts of believers to many revelations of knowledge and understanding, but speculations about a rapture theory never entered their teachings. In fact, the idea of a pre-tribulation rapture did not creep into the light of day until early in the nineteenth century. We shall see that the rapture theory didn't appear on the world scene until 1812. We also will examine the parable of the Wheat and Tares, which shows us in elegant simplicity that rapturist doctrine is exactly the opposite of the teachings of our Lord concerning the epic events that will transpire at the end of the age.

From the very beginning, rapture doctrines have brought strife to the body of Christ, leaving a legacy of turmoil that continues to this day. The contrast between the confusion caused by error and the unity inspired by truth becomes evident when we consider the warm reception given to the apostle Paul when he taught doctrinal revelation to his brothers at Jerusalem.

Fourteen years after his first trip to Jerusalem, Paul, accompanied by Barnabas and Titus, returned to the city for a visit with certain of the disciples. The teachings of Paul and his friends during this visit were certainly controversial in the context of the times, but the leaders of the local body received both message and messengers in a spirit of love for truth that only sound doctrine can inspire. Peter, James and John extended the right hand of fellowship to their brothers.[71]

The genesis of the pre-tribulation rapture theory was quite contrary to this biblical example. Rapturist founders were unwilling to extend the hand of fellowship to one another. Instead, they slipped rapidly into contention and division. The four propagators of this new doctrine were in disagreement from the outset. The four shaky pillars of the rapture doctrine were Emmanuel Lucanza, Margaret MacDonald, Edward Irving and Robert Norton. An examination of the diverse tangents of

71 Note in Galatians 2:2 that Paul states, "I went up by revelation."

their lines of thought tells us much about the cracked foundations upon which today's futurists and rapturists stand.

Let me briefly insert a chronology of date setters. If the rapture doctrine isn't bad enough, these speculators have set themselves up above the knowledge of God, attempting to go where Christ Himself would not venture! They have futilely attempted to date our Lord's second appearing. It is amazing how many Christians continually fall for this spectacle of scholastic manipulation!

Tichonius 381	**Irvingites of England 1864**
Hippolytus and Lactanius 500	**Hans Wood 1880**
Joachim of Floris 1260	**Mother Shipton 1881**
Michael Stiefel 1533	**Joanna Southcott 1884**
Isaac Newton 1715	**Charles Taze Russell 1914**
William Whiston 1734	**Edward D. Griffin 1921**
Johann Albrecht Bengel 1836	**Joseph F. Rutherford 1925**
William Miller 1834	**William Branham 1977**
Joseph Wolff 1847	**Edgar C. Whisenat 1988**
Philo Britannicus 1849	

But of that day and hour knoweth no man...[72]

The Coming of Messiah in Glory and Majesty, a book by Emmanuel Lacuna (1731-1801), a Jesuit priest from Chile who spent his last years in Spain and Italy, contains what some say is the first known reference to this strange new idea of rapture. Elliott contends that this book was probably written about 1791, around the outbreak of the French Revolution. He states that a criticism was written on the work by Fra Pablo de la Conception, of the Carmelite Convent in Cadiz.[73] However, Elliott does not mention the rapture theory when examining Lacunza's treatise. David MacPherson states, "At least one writer has suggested that this 1812 work originated the two-stage Rapture theory, but an examination of Lacunza's words rules out any such conclusions."[74] MacPherson cited two references, Duncan McDougall in *The Rapture of the Saints*, pp. 15, 31, and *Old Fashioned Prophecy Magazine*, revised edition, 1970. MacPherson's contention is that Lacunza's notion that the shout, voice of the archangel, and trump of God will occur "much before His arrival

72 Matthew 24:36

73 E.B. Elliott, Horae Apocalypticae, Vol 4, p. 513

74 David MacPherson, The Unbelievable Pre-Tribulation Origin, p. 38-9.

on earth" hardly resembles two-stage rapturism. Who knows? MacPherson may be right. Nevertheless, Lacunza's book was published in Spain and then translated into English and published in London in 1827. His posthumous book tumbled into the stream of theological discourse on an apparent wave of deception. The book was attributed to a fictitious author named Rabbi Juan Josafat Ben-Ezra. In an extensive introduction, the translator Rev. Edward Irving contended that the book was the work of a converted Jew!

Rev. Irving (1792-1834), a presbyter of the Church of Scotland, embraced the theory of a pre-tribulation rapture after reading Lacunza's manuscript. It wasn't long before others began to follow his lead.

> *Knowing fully well that he was giving the body of Christ a false position on the second coming of Christ and the resurrection of the dead, he presented Lacunza's work as a new revelation from God. Irving became one of the most eloquent preachers of his time. In 1828 his open air meetings in Scotland drew crowds of ten thousand people. In March 1830, he held a series of prophecy meetings in which he introduced Lacunza's ideas.*[75]

In 1830 in Port Glasgow, Scotland, a 15-year-old named Margaret MacDonald claimed she had received a new revelation in a vision, then set about to share this vision of a pre-tribulation rapture with anyone who would listen. One who did was Robert Norton (1807-1883), who recorded Margaret's prophecies and published them in a book, *The Restoration of Apostles and Prophets in the Catholic Apostolic Church* (London, 1861). I don't know whether history records Margaret reading or hearing of Irving's translation of Lacuna. Norton would later write that Miss MacDonald was the first to advance the idea of pre-tribulation rapture.[76]

The rapturist doctrine of today, which claims that every believer will be taken away before a terrible time of wrath and judgment, is quite different from the fragments of rapture that Lacunza, MacDonald and Norton touted. These nineteenth century believers proclaimed a partial rapture in which only a select portion of the body of believers would be chosen. The identity of the select portion quickly became a focal point of confusion and disagreement.

Lacunza claimed that only those believers who partake of the sacra-

75 Michael J. Berry, Foundation for Restoration, p. 63-4.

76 I reference the reader to three excellent investigations of pretribuation rapture teaching: John L. Bray, The Origin of the PreTribulation Rapture Teaching; Dave MacPherson, The Unbelievable Pre-Thibulation Origin; and Ralph Woodrow, Great Prophecies of the Bible, Part One: "The Second Coming of Christ."

ment of the Eucharist would be raptured; Miss MacDonald said the rapture would take away only those who were filled with the Spirit; and Norton claimed that only Christians who were sealed by the Holy Ghost with the laying on of hands would be raptured. What a mess!

These were the fragments which men began to scrutinize, rearrange, and expand upon as they wrestled with this novel idea. Denominations and congregations examined it. A few embraced the prospect of escape (as defined in this context), but most rejected it as contrary to God's Word. It took a disgruntled cleric of the Church of England to guide pre-tribulation rapture teaching into the mainstream of prophetic interpretation.

John Nelson Darby (1880-1882), who was ordained a deacon by the Church of England in 1825, was acquainted with Edward Irving and had visited Miss MacDonald in the days when she was having her visions. The potential of their radical new prophecy of a rapture intrigued Darby, who was already unhappy with the lethargic conditions prevailing in many churches of his time. The pre-tribulation rapture theory became the rallying point of Darby's break from the Church of England and the focus of his ascent to a position of leadership in the Plymouth Brethren movement.

The Plymouth Brethren were an offshoot of the Brethren in Ireland, a diverse group of dissidents who first considered the pre-tribulation rapture in their annual Powerscourt prophetic conference in 1833. Darby took the lead as the chief spokesman for this new eschatological theory, which aroused great controversy. To many, it was evident that Darby's teachings were extremely contrary to the historic Christian faith, causing scores of his followers and associates to depart from him. Some were actually excommunicated because of their opposition to Darby's teachings. Men such as the great "Prince of Preachers," Charles H. Spurgeon, and George Mueller would have nothing to do with these new theories.

Darby visited America seven times and exerted tremendous influence in developing the Brethren movement in this county. His views on the rapture theory received widespread notoriety when Cyrus Ingerson Scofield incorporated them in the *Scofield Reference Bible* in 1909.

Scofield (1843-1921), a Congregational minister whose rapturist ideas were influenced by the thought of J.H. Brooks and Malechi Taylor (a member of the Brethren movement), became one of Darby's most enthusiastic promoters. The Scofield Bible has influenced countless thousands of believers.

It is interesting to note that the majority of Scofield's contemporaries—

men such as Charles R. Eerdman, W.G. Moorhead, A.J. Gordon and Nathaniel West—rejected the views of this new British doctrine.

Today, students of Bible prophecy are turning away from this view. The endless date-setting throughout the decade of the 1980's has awakened many to the folly of dispensationalism and turned their hearts to search for prophetic truth.

I hope this brief chronology will encourage you to question the roots of many of the prophetic teachings you have been taught. Remember, if the root is bad, how much more rotten will the fruit be!

Now let us turn to the Scriptures and discover whether or not this new teaching is compatible with Holy Writ. We first will examine our Lord's parable and interpretation concerning the tares and the wheat, which deals with the Church's position in the world at the end of the age.

Scriptural Refutation

Following is the parable of the Tares and the Wheat as recorded in Matthew 13:24-30.

v.24 Another parable put he forth unto them, saying, The kingdom of heaven is likened unto a man which sowed good seed in his field:

v.25 But while men slept, his enemy came and sowed tares among the wheat, and went his way.

v.26 But when the blade was sprung up, and brought forth fruit, then appeared the tares also.

v.27 So the servants of the householder came and said unto him, Sir, didst not thou sow good seed in thy field? from whence then hath it tares?

v.28 He said unto them, An enemy hath done this. The servants said unto him, Wilt thou then that we go and gather them up?

v.29 But he said, Nay; lest while ye gather up the tares, ye root up also the wheat with them.

v.30 Let both grow together until the harvest: and in the time of harvest I will say to the reapers, Gather ye together first the tares, and bind them in bundles to burn them: but gather the wheat into my barn.

Our Lord interpreted the parable in verses 36-43 of the same chapter.

v.36 Then Jesus sent the multitude away, and went into the house: and his disciples came unto him, saying, Declare unto us the parable of the tares of the field.

v.37 He answered and said unto them, He that soweth the good seed is the Son of man;

v.38 The field is the world; the good seed are the children of the kingdom; but the tares are the children of the wicked one;

v.39 The enemy that sowed them is the devil; the harvest is the end of the world; and the reapers are the angels.

v.40 As therefore the tares are gathered and burned in the fire [first], so shall it be in the end of this world.

v.41 The Son of man shall send forth his angels, and they shall gather out of his kingdom all things that offend, and them which do iniquity;

v.42 And shall cast them into a furnace of fire: there shall be wailing and gnashing of teeth.

v.43 Then shall the righteous shine forth as the sun in the kingdom of their Father...

Think of this Scripture as it relates to the pre-tribulation rapturists who are telling us that the Church will be gone for seven (or three and a half) years before the end of the age. But what did our Lord say? "Let them both grow together until the harvest" (v. 30). We read that not only are they both to grow together until the end of the harvest, but also that our Lord in His interpretation states definitely that the "harvest" is the consummation of the age.

In His parable and interpretation, Jesus unquestionably states that the wicked are gathered first! Such is His divine sequence of events. Are we to inherit and rule the earth forever? Yes, we are (Rev. 2:26-27). Were the wicked destroyed from the earth in Noah's time? Yes, they were (Matt. 24:37).

This truth of God dealing first with the wicked in the first resurrection caused great embarrassment to men who separate these two events (the resurrection and the revelation) by several years. (Note: Students who seek deeper insight into the truth about the end of the age are directed to Alexander Reese's book, *The Approaching Advent of Christ,* which in my opinion, is the most scholarly refutation of pre-tribulation rapture teaching currently in print.)

Other serious discrepancies between rapturist theory and biblical truth are made evident in the story of Martha and Lazarus. Martha believed that her brother Lazarus would "rise in the resurrection at the last day" (John 11:24). The truth could not be any plainer. The last day of this present age is when the righteous shall be resurrected, not seven or three and half years prior.

Job, the Old Testament saint, also taught that the dead would not rise until "the heavens be no more." Job 14:10-12 says:

v.10 But man dieth, and wasteth away: yea, man giveth up the ghost, and where is he?

v.11 As the waters fail from the sea, and the flood decayeth and drieth up:

v.12 So man lieth down, and riseth not: till the heavens be no more, they shall not awake, nor be raised out of their sleep.

In the Book of Daniel, the rapturists are faced with another very difficult situation. In Daniel 7:25 we read, "And he [the antichrist] shall speak great words against the most High, and shall wear out [persecute and prevail against] the saints of the most High..." How can the Antichrist persecute the saints if they are raptured before this period?[77] These questions and their answers must be faced when we deal with a misdirected, but influential, escape mentality.

Let's look at another difficult situation for the rapturist teachers. The word "secret" is often used in their writings to describe the pre-tribulation rapture. But does your Bible teach you that the resurrection (the proper term for the rapture) will be secret, invisible, and even a quiet event? Consider the following verse, First Thessalonians 4:16: "For the Lord himself shall descend from heaven with a shout, with the voice of the archangel, and with the trump of God..."

To me, this indicates anything but a secret rapture. It doesn't matter whether we look at this in a figurative or literal sense. "Shout," "voice," and "trump" indicate a loud, noisy, visible and open return of our Lord. The Scripture says, "Every eye shall see him." Jesus warned us against teaching that His coming was to be a secret event.

Surely this is thought-provoking evidence concerning this matter. The idea of two comings is at best frivolity and at worst deliberate fabrication. If the ministry had not neglected the historically prominent Protestant interpretation of Bible prophecy (Historical School), they would not be in the embarrassing and targeted situation in which they find themselves today! Ministers who are searching for truth in relation to the Kingdom of God are finding it very difficult to remain futurist in their eschatology and dispensationalist in their views of the Kingdom and the true Israel.

77 The dynastic papal Antichrist fulfilled this prophecy during the Dark Ages. Just short of 13 centuries (1260 years), Rome prevailed against her enemies just as the Scriptures prophesied she would. The dispensationalist teaching that Antichrist is yet to come and fulfill this prophecy is wrong! Ribera did not have the keys of knowledge; instead, he slammed shut the door of understanding.

Part Six
And a Kingdom

My Position

Daniel 7:14

And there was given him [Christ] dominion, and glory, and a kingdom, that all people, nations, and languages, should serve him: his dominion is an everlasting dominion, which shall not pass away, and his kingdom that which shall not be destroyed.

Luke 22:29

And I appoint [covenant] unto you a kingdom, as my Father hath appointed [covenanted] unto me...

Matthew 21:43

Therefore say I unto you, The kingdom of God shall be taken from you, and given to a nation bringing forth the fruits thereof

Historically, there has always been controversy regarding the Kingdom of God. If one reads his Bible, he cannot but perceive that the message of the Kingdom is a powerful ongoing theme. For instance, it is agreed upon by most, that the fifth kingdom, or Stone Kingdom, mentioned in the above quote from Daniel, is none other than Christ's Kingdom. It is implied in this verse, because of the people, nations and languages involved, that the kingdom is upon the earth. In apparent contrast, Jesus is quoted in the Gospels as saying, "My Kingdom is not of this world."[78] How can we reconcile these apparent contradictions? The prophet Daniel states that Christ will set up a Kingdom which is full of peoples, various nations and languages which, according to the text, must be a kingdom upon this earth. However, Jesus says that it is not of this world, the implication being that it will be anywhere but on this earth. Is our God the author of confusion? To make this even more interesting, Jesus said that His Kingdom would "suffer violence!"[79] Therefore, if Christ's Kingdom presently is restricted to Heaven, how can Heaven, already purged of angelic wickedness, be violent if it is only possessed by saved saints? I read in the parable of the Wheat and Tares that "The son of man shall send forth his angels, and they shall gather out of his kingdom all things that offend..."[80] I think I am raising a fair point. Jesus instructs His disciples to teach people to pray that this King-

78 John 18:36

79 Matthew 11:12

80 Matthew 13:41

dom would come, and that His will be done on earth as it is in Heaven.

Our Bible is full of teachings concerning kingdoms; there are over three hundred examples. Not all of these are in reference to God's Kingdom. However, with this much teaching on kingdoms, specifically on why some prospered and others failed, it can be safely assumed that God wants us to understand something about kingdom principles. If the Church teaches that the Kingdom is restricted to heavenly places, or is only within our hearts, how can the saints possess a Kingdom that lingers in the clouds or the hearts of men? (See Daniel 7:18-24.)

Christ's disciples were intrigued concerning the message of the Kingdom. Jesus answered their inquiries with wonderful parables. "The Kingdom of God is like unto..." He described it, for example, in terms of a field being the world. I have a question for my dispensationalist friends. What parable describes the Kingdom as a place totally restricted to the heavens? Can you find one that even hints at such a thing? I can find it described as a merchant, field, a great treasure... The disciples had the audacity to ask the Lord if He would restore the Kingdom to Israel during their lifetime! If all Jesus taught was a spiritual Kingdom, why would the disciples be entertaining such earthly impressions?

If one were to pursue a systematic study, researching all the references to the Kingdom of Heaven and the Kingdom of God, he would be forced to come to the overwhelming conclusion that the consistent theme of our Lord's Kingdom is "earthly manifestation." I do not know how one could come to any other conclusion.

An appropriate question: What is a Kingdom? We could say that it consists of a king, those who obey him (his subjects), his laws, and an area of land (real estate). I believe this is a logical conclusion, consistent with biblical teaching. All Christians would agree on who our King is, but after that we enter into debate.

The majority of Bible scholars teach that there will be a Kingdom on this earth. Only a minority teach that the Kingdom, in totality, will be spiritual. The Bible teaches us about many spiritual things, such as gifts, songs, drinks, and bodies, but I don't think Christ's Kingdom is without physical manifestation.

I am not saying that the Kingdom is presently in a perfect state. Remember that Jesus stated that "the field is the Kingdom wherein grow both wheat and tares." Again, how can tares ascend into a heavenly Kingdom which is specifically reserved for the saints? The Bible even goes further and teaches us that Christ will rule the Kingdom with a rod of iron. Who will be subject to this rod of iron—the wheat? No, iron will beat down the tares.

"My kingdom is not of this world," Jesus said. He was right. The authority of His Kingdom is not presently granted (recognized) by this world. The preposition "of" in the above verse is properly translated "origin." Jesus simply says that His authority did not originate from this world's systems. This is what he was telling Pilate when questioned about His Kingship (John 18:37).

David said, "The Lord hath prepared his throne in the heavens, and his kingdom ruleth over all" (Ps. 103:19). Christ clearly prayed, "...Thy kingdom come. Thy will be done in earth, as it is in heaven" (Matt. 6:10). Jesus understood where the Father wanted His Kingdom to be manifested—on earth! Was this Kingdom to be manifested in one glorious event, or was it to start as a little stone and progressively grow to someday fill the whole earth?

> *And in the days of these kings shall the God of heaven set up a kingdom, which shall never be destroyed: and the kingdom shall not be left to other people, but it shall break in pieces and consume all these kingdoms, and it shall stand for ever (Dan. 2:44).*

Growth Principle

It would be easy to show that at our present rate of progress the kingdoms of this world never could become the kingdom of our Lord and of His Christ. Indeed, many in the Church are giving up the idea of it except on the occasion of the advent of Christ, which, as it chimes in with our own idleness, is likely to be a popular doctrine. I myself believe that King Jesus will reign, and the idols be utterly abolished; but I expect the same power which turned the world upside down once will still continue to do it. The Holy Ghost would never suffer the imputation to rest upon His holy name that He was not able to convert the world.

Charles H. Spurgeon

A century ago Spurgeon uttered these prophetic words of warning to the Church. His perception of "idleness" and the encompassing doctrines which would seek to justify such positions should be heeded by this present age, and any generation yet to follow. After examining the present truth of the Kingdom in the previous section, we must now establish this Kingdom's prophesied "growth principle," which is exactly what Spurgeon was talking about. And then we must face serious questions that will be answered only by the continual unfolding of true prophetic biblical interpretation. Eschatological teachings must not contradict Kingdom principles of growth and dominion.

The Kingdom of God can be defined from several justifiable points of view, and I recognize that. However, I came across one very interesting and biblically accurate definition:

The Kingdom of God is the sovereign rule of God manifested in Christ to defeat His enemies, creating a people over whom He reigns, and issuing in a realm or realms in which the power of His reign is experienced.[81]

I thought the emphasis on defeating Christ's enemies was very appropriate. I believe this is what the Scriptures teach. I can't find anywhere the Scriptures teaching the triumph of an end-time Antichrist. Friends, this is the very danger of dispensationalism. If our eschatological teaching is perverted by Ribera's theories, then we are forced into a difficult realm of confusion. If we believe that Daniel 7:21, which states, "I beheld, and the same horn made war with the saints, and prevailed against them," is yet to occur in the future under Hal Lindsey's (Ribera's) end-time

81 The Zondervan Topical Bible, p. 608.

Antichrist, then why build for the future? All our endeavors will be prevailed against by the Man of Sin. Protestant Historicism teaches, and systematically reveals, that this event was already fulfilled during the papacy's 1,260 years of dominion and "wearing out"[82] of the Church. This was a period of time in which over fifty million people were put to death because they refused to bow to the medieval harlot church. God has not forgotten, and Rome has never repented! But thank God that His Kingdom is destined to grow, without interruption or escape, until the epipehaneia of His parousia, "the brightness of his coming."[83]

Daniel records one of the most graphic prophecies relating to the principle of growth and dominion in chapter two.

> *v.34 Thou sawest till that a stone was cut out without hands, which smote the image upon his feet that were of iron and clay, and brake them to pieces.*
>
> *v.35 ...and the stone that smote the image became a great mountain, and filled the whole earth.*

Stone................................ becomes........................... MOUNTAIN

It does not take a great theologian to interpret this simple verse. Christ's Kingdom grows and grows and grows until the earth is filled! And once the earth is filled, it will be ruled by Kingdom principles, enforced, if necessary, by a rod of iron. Jesus said, "If I cast out devils by the Spirit of God then the kingdom of God is come unto you." (Matt. 12:28) Could it be that this authority will prevail and fill the earth? The authority of a "present growing Kingdom!" This authority is able to "cast down imaginations, and every high thing that exalteth itself against the knowledge of God."[84] Christ said all authority was given to Him. Will a kingdom yet to come have more authority than His present Kingdom has? Did Jesus partially equip His Church, or is it, as Spurgeon declares, "the same power which turned the world upside down once will still continue to do it?" In my opinion, the answers are very obvious, unless one is looking through a futurist veil. "Do you not know that the Christians will one day judge and govern the world?"[85]

Our Lord taught us two very powerful parables about His Kingdom and its growth principle. The first is the parable of the mustard seed:

---

82 Daniel 7:25

83 II Thessalonians 2:8

84 II Corinthians 10:5

85 I Corinthians 6:2, Amplified Bible

Matthew 13:31-32

...The kingdom of heaven is like to a grain of mustard seed, which a man took, and sowed in his field: which indeed is the least of all seeds: but when it is grown, it is the greatest among herbs, and becometh a tree, so that the birds of the air come and lodge in the branches thereof

This seed is destined to mature and dominate all the other herbs. Such is the destiny of Christ's victorious Church. There is no force on earth that can hinder its growth. In the parable of the leaven, Jesus taught that the effectiveness of His Kingdom is not restricted to parts of the meal (earth), but rather it is going to leaven the "whole"—the entire earth.

Matthew 13:33

Another parable spake he unto them; The kingdom of heaven is like unto leaven, which a woman took, and hid in three measures of meal, till the whole was leavened.

Our Lord is uttering "things which have been kept secret from the foundation of the world."[86] He has revealed them; why must His Church still be in the dark about such basic issues? I pray that the veil be hastily torn away and the concept of conquering is restored to the ministry.

So what am I saying? The truth of the Kingdom is being hindered by dispensationalism. The knowledge of its progressive growth toward ultimate triumph is shattered by the teachers of futuristic Bible prophecy. The Church's potential is hindered by the philosophy, "Why polish the brass on a sinking ship?" According to the parable of the leaven, we are going to permeate every aspect of society and cast down all that exalts itself above the laws of our magnificent Savior. Remember, until all these exaltations (enemies) of Christ are put under His feet (the body), He will remain in the heavens![87]

---

86 Matthew 13:35

87 Acts 3:21

The Complete Restoration

Acts 3:20-21 The Amplified New Testament:

v.20 And that He may send [to you] the Christ, the Messiah, Who before was designated and appointed for you, Jesus,

v.21 Whom heaven must receive [and retain] until the time for the complete restoration of all that God spoke by the mouth of all His holy prophets for ages past—from the most ancient time in the memory of man.

It never ceases to amaze me how so many teachers have overlooked this very important verse of Scripture when they expounded on our Lord's Second Coming. The implications are immediately evident, and they are reinforced by other biblical testimonies which we will examine. The challenge is immense, and I don't intend to tackle it in its entirety. "Complete restoration of all that God spoke by the mouth of all His holy prophets!" What did all the prophets proclaim which must be totally restored before Christ is released from the heavens? I will not try to systematically define that; however, I can present one of the most obvious and dynamic admonitions pertaining to this requirement—the destruction of Christ's enemies.

Dennis Peacocke, founder of Strategic Christian Services, wrote recently concerning what he expected to emerge in future prophetic scenarios. He said:

1 believe God has clearly spoken to my spirit twice in the last fifteen years in terms of the future and the Church's place in it. In 1976, I was told by the Lord two things: 1) that there would be "at least as many surprises around My Second Coming as there were around my First," and 2) that "when My people need to clearly understand these things, I will reveal them." In 1988, I received what I believe to be another clear word: "Tell My people that they have time to obey Me."[88]

I think Peacocke is correct. Acts 3:21 alone is a noteworthy surprise to many prophetic dispensationalists. How can a teaching that portrays the Bride of Christ as a powerless entity needing rescue before the terrible Antichrist appears be reconciled with the biblical proclamation of "total restoration" imparted to a victorious Church, which actually is the signal that His appearing is eminent? Likewise, consider the time

88 Dennis Peacocke, The Rebuilder; April 1990.

factor. The dispensationalists had the Church in a "hurry up offence," to quote Peacocke, confident that Christ would return before a forty-year period expired. This is a reference to their teaching that, within the span of a generation after the birth of the nation of Israel in 1948, Christ must return. Well, we're still here. In your opinion, is the New Testament Church totally restored to even first century apostolic power, authority and understanding? I'll let you be honest before God while contemplating that issue. Furthermore, are all Christ's enemies under His feet? Must this happen before He returns? Remember, we are the possessors of the feet.

David proclaimed in the 110th Psalm:

v.1 The Lord said unto my Lord, Sit thou at my right hand, until I make thine enemies thy footstool.

Likewise the writer of the epistle to the Hebrews admonished in chapter ten:

v.I2 But this man, after he had offered one sacrifice of sins for ever, sat down on the right hand of God;

v.13 From henceforth expecting [waiting] till his enemies be made his footstool.

In the mouth of two witnesses a thing can be established. This truth of all enemies ultimately being put under the feet of the Church is clearly proclaimed in Scripture. Paul said that the God of peace would bruise (crush) satan under our feet! (Rom. 16:20) Until this occurs, the heavens must retain the Christ, according to the Word of God. We can get angry about it and retain our traditional teachings, or we can believe what the Word says!

In commenting on the phrase, "till his enemies be made his footstool," one commentator expounded eloquently the magnitude of the claim:

Till all that oppose his high priesthood and sacrificial offering shall be defeated, routed, and confounded; and acknowledge in their punishment, the supremacy of his power as universal and eternal King, who refused to receive him as their atoning and sanctifying priest.[89]

When all of Christ's enemies have bowed their knees to His authority, then, or in the events which bring this to pass, He will return and resurrect the dead in Christ and translate the living righteous who have made themselves ready.[90]

89 Adam Clarke, Clarke's Commentary, Hebrews 10:13, p. 754:5.

90 I Thessalonians 4:16-17 and Revelation 19:7

I am not mocking the "promise of his coming,"[91] but rather proclaiming this coming as the Scriptures teach! When looking into the future we have a tendency to be fanciful and to speculate. We can only see the future in part. We must walk toward it by faith. However, we can walk in the right direction. And when these things unfold around us, we can then begin to accurately interpret them. We have a great example of this principle given in the Gospel of Matthew, chapter two.

In this chapter we are told the story of the wise men from the east who appeared before Herod, inquiring about the King of the Jews. They openly proclaimed His birth. Herod, being troubled, gathered the entire Sanhedrin and demanded understanding pertaining to this matter. This is probably occurring in the year 2 B.C. Let's put ourselves in Herod's time and listen to the Scriptures that are cited in reference to this proclaimed and expected Messiah.

First, Micah 5:2 is read, which identifies the town in which Christ would be born—Bethlehem (Matt. 2:5). Secondly, Matthew references Hosea 11:1, which reveals that the Messiah would be called out of Egypt (Matt. 2:15). And thirdly, he states that the prophets had proclaimed Him to be a Nazarene (Matt. 2:23). I have a question for you. If you were standing in the company of the Sanhedrin and this revelation were presented to you, do you think you could have accurately interpreted it? I doubt it. But the interpretation would be clear after it was fulfilled: Christ was born in Bethlehem and fled from Herod's wrath to Egypt. After Herod's death He returned to Nazareth, thus becoming a Nazarene, thereby fulfilling a seemingly confusing and contradicting prophecy. This is a lesson in prophetic interpretation that we must never forget. Look cautiously toward the future, and proclaim that which has already been perfectly fulfilled with absolute confidence in the credibility of our God and His prophetic word. Anticipate God the Father putting all enemies under Christ's feet.

---

91 II Peter 3:4

Conclusion

"Lord who hath believed our report?" wrote the apostle Paul to the Roman church. The issues discussed in this book are emerging as focal points of debate within the body of Christ, and I believe rightly so. Truth has always been a great issue with our God. There is a spirit of truth and a spirit of error. Both are destined to magnify themselves, thus having enormous ramifications. Any sea captain can tell you that a minor error in navigation can lead to disastrous results. Once one is off course he progressively widens his margin of error. I served for ten years as a United States Marine. I qualified on the rifle range many times. Part of our qualification process was shooting at targets five hundred yards away. There was no room for error. If your breathing was wrong, or there was a slight jerk of the trigger, you missed the target. If the target were ten feet in front of you it wouldn't make any difference. But as time and space enlarged, the round would continue on an erroneous course, eventually proving itself useless. In 1826, S.R. Maitland knocked the Protestants just a little off course, and now look how far we have strayed from prophetic truth. Futuristic eschatology is basically useless. It does not assert the credibility of the written Word; it mocks it.

We have seen how the truth of the seventy weeks has discredited the Jesuit theologians who fathered it and the Protestant dispensationalists who embraced it. But how does Judaism respond to it? Their own prophet Daniel proclaimed that Messiah the Prince (their Redeemer) came within five centuries of Artaxerxes' decree! How can they still reject Jesus? Adam Clarke summed up the obvious truth of this matter.

> *Daniel's weeks had so clearly defined the time of the true Messias, his coming, that the minds of the whole nation were raised into the expectation of him. Hence, it was doubted [inquired] of the Baptist, whether he were not the Messias, Luke iii. 15. Hence, it was, that the Jews are gathered together from all countries unto Jerusalem, Acts ii., expecting and coming to see, because at that time the term of revealing the Messias, that had been prefixed by Daniel, was come. Hence it was that there was so great a number of false Christs. Matt. xxiv. 5, & c., taking the occasion of their impostures hence, that now the time of that great expectation was at hand, and fulfilled: and in one word, They thought the kingdom of God should presently appear, Luke xix. 11.*
>
> *But when those times of expectation were past, nor did such a Mes-*

sias appear as they expected, (for when they saw the true Messias, they would not see him,) they first broke out into various, and those wild, conjectures coming to nothing, all ended in the curse (the just cause of their eternal blindness), "May their soul be confounded who compute the times!" They were fully aware that the time foretold by the prophets must be long since fulfilled; and that their obstinacy must be confounded by their own history, and the chronology of their own Scriptures; and therefore they have pronounced an anathema on those who shall attempt to examine, by chronological computations, the prophecies that predict his coming. Who can conceive a state of willful blindness or determine obstinacy superior to this![92]

Now what have I done with this salvo? No doubt I have opened myself to the charge of anti-Semitism. (This is always a risk for those who love the Jews enough to tell them the truth—salvation is by Christ or not at all, and when they do graft back in, it will be through Christ's blood, not the blood of bulls and goats which could never take away sins.) Likewise, Rome will call me a bigot, and Protestant fury will come from the fearful or compromising (ecumenical group) and label me a heretic. Character assassination always comes from those who cannot refute by Scripture or clear reason. It is to be expected. I am not contending with any man's person, but rather that which concerns words of truth.

What does a book like this do for the cause of unity? Hopefully it will help define its basis and requirements. But some may argue that Christ proclaimed a unity of the faith—not doctrine. That has been highly distorted. Paul admonished Timothy to "take heed unto thyself and unto the doctrine: continue in them..." (I Tim. 4:16) Men who will not fight for important Christian doctrines are those who refuse to obey Christ's directions in the Revelation. "Rise, and measure the temple [naos] of God..." The Temple is measured by His Word. "But the court which is without the temple leave out, [cast out] and measure it not..."[93] The commandment is clear; examine all doctrine by the Word. If it fails the test, cast it out. Futurism, dispensationalism and preterism have failed the test, so we must throw them out. Such doctrine has polluted Christ's holy Temple long enough!

I hope this exegetical perspective on one of the most important prophetic studies today facing the Church has been coherently presented. The truths and arguments presented will force an entire generation to rethink its eschatological positions. Nevertheless, this is only an intro-

92 Adam Clarke, Clarke Commentary, p. 45, Matthew 2:5

93 Revelation 11:1-2

duction to the whole matter. Teachings on the Book of Revelation must now be redefined, and many other portions of the written prophets, which have had their glorious prophecies "sealed" by strong error. True prophetic interpretation is the only weapon against the terrible curse of uncertainty running rampant in the ministry. Without understanding the true fulfillment of the seventy weeks, prophetic metaphor, the year-for-a-day principle, the Kingdom, restoration and Church history (to name a few vital principles), this goal cannot be achieved.

My heart burns within me in anticipation of seeing the glory of God's Word asserted upon the credibility of His written prophets. No doubt Christ is preparing a well-armed ministry to repair this terrible breach in the study of Bible prophecy.

There are many reasons why men are teaching on sinking sand, and truth will further expose their teachings. It is the Berean spirit that will wax valiant and victorious in this struggle. Once again men and women will require their teachers to "prove all things,"[94] and they, in turn, will search the Scriptures daily to determine whether these things be so.

The time has come for an open seminar and forum in the body of Christ concerning these issues. Truth does not leave a middle ground. It is time to throw down the gauntlet. The die is cast. I pray that men of God will have the courage to face this issue and stand strong against the ecumenical spirit of the one who sits on the Tiber.

I know who you are, and I refuse to look for another!

Like travelers, when they see their native soil, Writers rejoice to terminate their toil.

---

94 I Thessalonians 5:21

Appendix

I have deemed it necessary to include in this book a section citing some of the greatest thinkers of the English Reformation. The topic of the papal Antichrist arose several times in the course of this writing, yet I am aware that this book lacks a meticulous systematic teaching on the subject. The topic of the Papacy and the Antichrist is exhaustively covered in my book, ***The Present Reign of Jesus Christ***. A Berean student of history should have no problem researching this consistent historical theology, more often universally agreed upon than not in the Protestant church. Today, it is hard for us to comprehend this. We have the futurists to thank for that. The historical school has so often been overlooked, and its voluminous teaching misrepresented, that any man or woman who dares to proclaim it as the true interpretation faces the same intolerant and indignant spirits that these mighty English reformers faced. We must search far and wide to find teachers today who possess the capacity and courage of the Reformation fathers. I'm not talking about revelation knowledge, but rather intestinal fortitude and the ability to wield a razor-sharp sword of truth, no matter what the cost!

TYNDALE (Martyred 1536)

Now, though the Bishop of Rome and his sects give Christ these names, [Jesus, a Savior, Christus, King appointed over all men, Emmanuel, God with us, Sanctus, that is, holy, that halloweth, sanctifieth, and blesseth all nations,] yet in that they rob him of the effect, and take the significations of his names unto themselves, and make of him but a hypocrite, as they themselves be, they be the right Antichrists, and deny both the Father and the Son; for they deny the witness the Father bare unto the Son, and deprive the Son of all the power and glory that his Father gave him.[95]

CRANMER (Archbishop of Canterbury, 1533; martyred 1555)

But the Romish Antichrist, to deface this great benefit of Christ, hath taught that his sacrifice upon the cross is not sufficient hereunto, without another sacrifice devised by him, and made by the priest; or else without indulgences, beads, pardons, pilgrimages, and such pelfry, to supply Christ's imperfection: and that Christian people cannot apply to themselves the benefits of Christ's passion, but that the same is in the distribution of the bishop of Rome; or else that by Christ we have no full remission, but be delivered only from sin, and yet remaineth the

95 Tyndales Works, vol. ii. p. 183. (Parker Ed)

temporal pain in purgatory due for the same; to be remitted after this life by the Romish Antichrist and his ministers, who take upon them to do for us that thing which Christ either would not or could not do. O heinous blasphemy, and most detestable injury against Christ! ***O wicked abomination in the temple of God!*** [emphasis mine] O pride intolerable of Antichrist, and most manifest token of the ***Son of Perdition***; extolling himself above God, and with Lucifer exalting his seat and power above the throne of God![96]

LATIMER (Bishop of Worcester, 1535-1539; martyred 1555)

Judge not before the Lord's coming. In this we learn to know Antichrist, which doth elevate himself in the Church, and judgeth at his pleasure before the time. His canonizations, and judging of men before the Lord's judgment, be a manifest token of Antichrist. How can he know saints? He knoweth not his own heart.[97]

RIDLEY (Bishop of Rochester 1547, and of London, 1550-1553; martyred 1555)

The see [of Rome] is the seat of Satan; and the bishop of the same, that maintaineth the abominations thereof, is Antichrist himself indeed. And for the same causes this see at this day is the same which St. John calleth in his Revelation "Babylon" or "the whore of Babylon," and "spiritual Sodom and Egypt," "the mother of fornications and of the abominations upon the earth."[98]

HOOPER (Bishop of Gloucester, 1551-1554; martyred 1555)

If godly Moses and his brother Aaron never acclaimed this title [to be God's vicar and lieutenant] in the earth, doubtless it is a foul and detestable arrogancy, that these ungodly bishops of Rome attribute unto themselves to be the heads of Christ's Church…

Because God hath given this light unto my countrymen, which be all persuaded, (or else God send them to be persuaded), that [neither] the bishop of Rome, nor none other, is Christ's vicar upon the earth, it is no need to use any long or copious oration: it is so plain that it needeth no probation: the very properties of Antichrist, I mean of Christ's great and principle enemy, is so openly known to all men that are not blinded with the smoke of Rome, that they know him to be the Beast that John describeth in the Apocalypse.[99]

96 Preface to Defence, &c, in Works of Archbishop Cranmer, Vol. i. pp. 5-7. (Parker Ed.)

97 "Third Sermon before Edward VI," in Works of Bishop Latimer, Vol. i, pp. 148-149. (Parker Ed.)

98 Farewell Letter, in Works of Bishop Ridley, p. 415. (Parker Ed.)

99 "Declaration of Christ," Ch. iii, in Writings of Bishop Hooper, pp. 22-24. (Parker Ed.)

PHILPOT (Archdeacon of Winchester; martyred 1555)

I doubt not but you have already cast the price of this your building of the house of God, that it is like to be no less than your life; for I believe (as Paul saith) that God hath appointed us in these latter days like sheep to the slaughter. Antichrist is come again; and he must make a feast to Beelzebub his father of many Christian bodies, for the restoring again of his kingdom. Let us watch and pray, that the same day may not find us unready.[100]

BRADFORD (Prebendary of St. Paul's; martyred 1555)

This word of God, written by the prophets and apostles, left and contained in the canonical books of the holy Bible, I do believe to contain plentifully "all things necessary to salvation," so that nothing, as necessary to salvation, ought to be added thereto... In testimony of this faith I render and give my life; being condemned, as well for not acknowledging the Antichrist of Rome to be Christ's Vicar-general, and supreme Head of his Catholic and Universal Church, here and elsewhere upon earth, as for denying the horrible and idolatrous doctrine of transubstantiation, and Christ's real, corporal, and carnal presence in his supper, under the forms and accidents of bread and wine.[101]

HOMILIES OF THE CHURCH OF ENGLAND (Authorized 1563)

Our Savior Christ and St. Peter teacheth, most earnestly and agreeably, obedience to kings, as to the chief and supreme rulers in this world, next under God. But the bishop of Rome teacheth that they that are under him are free from all burdens and changes of the commonwealth, and obedience towards their prince, most clearly against Christ's doctrine and St. Peter's. He ought therefore rather to be called Antichrist, and the successor of the Scribes and Pharisees, than Christ's vicar or St. Peter's successor; seeing that not only in this point, but also in other weighty matters of Christian religion—in matters of remission and forgiveness of sins, and of salvation—he teacheth so directly against both St. Peter and against our Savior Christ: who not only taught obedience to kings, but also practised obedience in their conversation and living; for we read that they both paid tribute to the king.[102]

Neither ought miracles to persuade us to do contrary to God's word; for the Scriptures have for a warning hereof foreshewed, that the kingdom of Antichrist shall be mighty "in miracles and wonders," to the

---

100 Letter to Robert Glover, in Writings of Archdeacon Philpot, p. 244. (Parker Ed.)

101 "Farewell to the City of London," in Writings of Bradford, p. 435. (Parker Ed.)

102 "Homily of Obedience," Part iii; Homilies, p. 114. (Ed. Corrie, Cambridge, 1850).

strong illusion of all the reprobate. But in this they pass the folly and wickedness of the Gentiles, that they honour and worship the relics and bones of our saints; which prove that they be mortal men and dead, and therefore no gods to be worshipped; which the Gentiles would never confess of their gods for very shame.[103]

The true Church…hath always three notes or marks whereby it is known; pure and sound doctrine, the sacraments ministered according to Christ's holy institution, and the right use of ecclesiastical discipline…. Now, if ye will compare this with the Church of Rome—not as it was in the beginning, but as it is presently, and hath been for the space of nine hundred years and odd—you shall well perceive the state thereof to be so far wide from the nature of the true Church, that nothing can be more… The Popes, in not hearing Christ's voice, as they ought to do, but preferring their own decrees before the express word of God, do plainly argue to the world that they are not of Christ, nor yet possessed with his spirit….They are worthily accounted among the number of false prophets and false Christs, which deceived the world a long while. The Lord of heaven and earth defend us from their tyranny and pride, that they never enter into his vineyard again …and of his great mercy so work in all men's hearts, by the mighty power of the Holy Ghost, that the comfortable gospel of his Son Christ may be truly preached, truly received, and truly followed in all places, to the beating down of sin, death, the pope, the devil, and all the kingdom of Antichrist![104]

JEWEL (Bishop of Salisbury, 1559-1571)

Such shall be the power and authority of Antichrist; so shall he possess the consciences of the people; so shall he sit as an idol in their hearts; so shall he stand in the place of God, and "show himself that he is God." The people shall receive his doctrine, and believe his word; they shall fall down before him, and worship him: they shall say, "Who is like unto the beast? what creature is so beautiful as he?" they shall honour him as God. But what is he which hath been called by the name of God?… who hath been so wicked? who hath ever so much forgotten himself? In what place hath he dwelt? or what hath he been?—Here methinketh I see the secret motions of your heart. You look that I should name the Bishop of Rome; that it is he which hath suffered himself to be called by the name of God. I will not tell you in mine own words. Unless the bishop himself so speak, I will not tell you… Then let us see what he hath written of himself, and what he hath suffered others to write. Pope

---

103 "Homily against Peril of Idolatry," part iii, Homilies, p. 234.

104 "Homily for Whitsunday," Part ii, Homilies, pp. 465, 466, 467, 471.

Nicholas saith… "It is well known that the Pope of the godly prince Constantine was called God." …In the Extravagants it is set down: Dominus Deus noster papa: "Our Lord God the Pope."[105] Mark these words: "Our Lord God the Pope." In them the Pope is called Lord, and is called God. O merciful Lord God, which from thy heavens beholdest this vanity, how great is thy mercy in suffering this! I devise not this. His own books, his own doctors, his own decrees and decretals speak it, and set it down: —Credere Dominum Deum nostrum papam non posuisse statuere, prout statuit, hereticum censeretur: "To believe that our Lord God the Pope might not decree as he decreed it were a matter of heresy." It is so written there: he hath heard it, he hath seen it, he knoweth it is so: yet he suffereth it to go abroad, and thereby suffereth himself to be called "God." He hath burnt many saints of God, and holy men, for no other cause but for the profession of the Gospel: he hath in many places burnt the Holy Bible, and such books as teach nothing but godliness. Where did he ever burn, (what speak I of burning?) where may it appear that ever he controlled any for so writing, or called in such speeches?[106]

Many places of the Holy Scripture, spoken of Antichrist, seemed in old times to be dark and doubtful; for that as then it appeared not unto what state and government they might be applied: but now, by the doctrine and practice of the Church of Rome, to them that have eyes to see, they are as clear and as open as the sun.[107]

We are not the ministers of Antichrist, Master Harding, but the witnesses of Christ. He is Antichrist, as St. Paul sheweth you, "that sitteth in the temple of God, and advanceth himself above all that is called God." And to speak more particularly of the matter, by St. Gregory's judgment he is Antichrist, or "the forerunner of antichrist, that calleth himself the universal bishop," and vaunteth himself as "the king of pride," and hath "an army of priests prepared for him," and setteth himself, as Lucifer, above all his brethren. These be the words of St. Gregory: by such colours he blazed out the kingdom of Antichrist. Of him Cardinal Franciscus Zabarella saith thus: "…The Pope doth what him listeth, yea, though it be unlawful, and is more than a God." This is Antichrist, Master Harding, by the judgment of the wise and godly: and the supporters of him, whosoever and wheresoever they be, are the ministers of Antichrist![108]

---

105 "Latterly the word Deum has been omitted." Ayre, On Jewel; Vol. i. p. 96.

106 Exposition of I Thessalonians ii. 4, in Works of Jewel, Vol. ii. p. 906-907. (Parker Ed.)

107 "Defence of the Apology"; Vol. iv. p. 744.

108 "Defence of the Apology," Part iv, ch. vi. div. 1, in Works of Bishop Jewel, Vol. iv. pp. 673-674.

BEACON (Chaplain to Archbishop Cranmer, and prebendary of Canterbury. Died 1567)

Antichrist hath set up divers sacrifices for sins, but namely that vile and abominable sacrifice of the mass, which he calleth a propitiatory, expiatory, and satisfactory sacrifice for the sins of the quick and the dead, necessary ***ad salutem***. This sacrifice he braggeth to be of like dignity, and of equal price, with that sacrifice which Christ the high and everlasting Bishop offered on the altar of the cross, yea, to be the very same: again, that he and his chaplains, in that sacrifice of the idolatrous mass, do daily offer up the Son of God to the Father of heaven for the daily sins of the people. Antichrist moreover is not ashamed to say that Christ, by the sacrifice of his death done on the altar of the cross, did only put away original sin; but he and his shavelings, by the sacrifice of their mass, putteth away, all other sins at all times, both actual, venial, mortal, & c.[109]

SANDYS (Bishop of Worester, 1559, of London, 1570, and Archbishop of York, 1576-1588)

Christ proposeth his heavenly treasures, remission of sins, justification, sanctification, mercy, grace, and salvation freely. He that "sitteth in the temple of God," and termeth himself Christ's Vicar, doth in like sort offer unto the people bread, water, wine, milk, pardon of sins, grace, mercy, and eternal life: but not freely. He is a merchant; he giveth nothing; and this is nothing which he selleth: for, although he makes large promises to the buyer, he selleth that which he hath not to deliver... Thus you see a manifest difference between Christ and Antichrist.[110]

FLUKE (Master of Pembroke Hall, Cambridge, 1557- 1589)

The second argument is, that Antichrist is called "the adversary"; and therefore is the greatest enemy of Christ, "denying Jesus Christ to be God and man, or to be our Mediator." I answer, the Pope doth so, denying the office of Christ; although, with the devils, he confess in words Jesus to be "the Holy One of God," and to be "Christ the Son of God..." His Divinity the Pope denieth by denying his only power in saving; his wisdom, in his word to be only sufficient; his goodness, in the virtue of his death to take away both pain and guilt of sin; which he arrogateth to himself by his blasphemous pardons. Christ's humanity he denieth by his transubstantiation; his mediation, in which he is principally Christ, he denieth by so many means of salvation as he maketh beside Christ; viz. man's merits, ceremonies invented by man, pardons, a new

109 "The Acts of Christ and of Antichrist," in Works of Beacon, Vol. iv. iii. p. 523. (Parker Ed.)

110 Sermons of Archbishop Sandy's, pp. 11-12. (Parker Ed.)

sacrifice of the mass, & c.

The city with seven hills is still the see of Antichrist described by St. John... The see being found, it is easy to find the person by St. Paul's description, and this note especially, that excludeth the heathen tyrants, "He shall sit in the temple of God." Which when we see to be fulfilled in the Pope, although none of the eldest fathers could see it, because it was performed after their death, we nothing doubt to say and affirm still, that the Pope is that "man of sin" and "son of perdition," the adversary that lifteth up himself "above all that is called God," and shall be destroyed "by the spirit of the Lord's mouth, and by the glory of his coming."[111]

WHITGIFT (Archbishop of Canterbury, 1583-1604)

For anything to be a note of Antichrist is not in the nature of any creature in itself; (for to that end nothing was made of God;) but it hangeth altogether of consenting to Antichrist's religion and the professing thereof. The which consent and profession being changed into the consent and profession of Christianity, there can stick in the things themselves no note or mark of Antichrist's religion. The use of bells was a mark of antichristianity in our churches, when the people by them were called to masses, and when they were rung against tempests. Now they are a token of Christianity, when the people by them are gathered together to the gospel of Christ and other holy actions.[112]

HOOKER (Master of the Temple; died 1600)

I permit it to your wise considerations, whether it be more likely, that as phrensy, though itself take away the use of reason, doth notwithstanding prove them reasonable creatures which have it, because none can be frantic but they—so antichristianity, being the bane and plain overthrow of Christianity, may nevertheless argue the church wherein Antichrist sitteth to be Christian. Neither have I ever hitherto heard or read any one word alleged of force to warrant, that God doth otherwise than so as hath been in the two next questions before declared bind himself to keep his elect from "worshipping the beast," and from "receiving his mark in their foreheads:" but he hath preserved and will preserve them from receiving any deadly wound at the hands of the Man of sin; whose deceit hath prevailed over none to death, but only such as "never loved the truth, such as took pleasure in unrighteousness." They in all ages whose hearts have delighted in the principal truth, and whose souls have thirsted after righteousness, if they received the mark of error, the

---

111 Flukes Answers, pp. 368,373. (Parker Ed.)

112 Whitgifts Defence of the Answer to the Admonition, Tract 7, ch. 5, div. 5, p. 276. (Lund. Bynneman, 1574.)

mercy of God, even erring, and dangerously erring, might save them: if they received the mark of heresy, the same mercy did, I doubt not, convert them.[113]

TRANSLATORS OF THE AUTHORIZED ENGLISH VERSION OF THE BIBLE (A.D. 1611)

Their contentment every day increaseth and taketh strength, when they observe that the zeal of your Majesty toward the house of God doth not slack or go backward, but is more and more kindled; manifesting itself abroad in the farthest parts of Christendom, by writing in defence of the truth; which hath given such a blow unto that Man of Sin as will not be healed.[114]

ARTICLES OF THE IRISH CHURCH (Agreed on by the Archbishops, Bishops, and the rest of the Clergy of Ireland, in Convocation at Dublin, A.D. 1615)

The Bishop of Rome is so far from being the supreme head of the universal Church of Christ, that his works and doctrine do plainly discover him to be that Man of Sin foretold in the Holy Scriptures, whom the Lord shall consume with the Spirit of his mouth, and shall abolish with the brightness of his coming.[115]

An Papa sit Antichristus, I hold ***affirmative***!

---

113 "Sermon on Justification," sect. 27, in Works of Hooker, Vol. iv. pp. 653-654. (Ed. Keble, Oxford 1836.)

114 Epistle Dedicatory to King James I.

115 Confession of Protestant Churches, p. 22 (Ed. Dublin, 1835.)